InQUIZition

InQUIZition

Q&A for the Curious Catholic and the Catholic Curious

by Patrick Madrid

2022

Copyright 2022 by Patrick Madrid.

Contents

Adventures in Theodicy 1

It's All Greek (or Latin, or Aramaic) to Me 8

Somebody Call a (Church) Doctor! 14

Is It Cheating if You Use Your Bible? 21

State of the Hypostatic Union 27

Very Clever! You Got Me Monologuing! 35

A Potpourri of Popery 40

Man and Wife, Say Man and Wife 46

Founders Keepers 53

In a World of Churches, Be a Cathedral 61

Holy Dynamic Duos! 68

Bears Beat Boys and Battlestar Galactica 75

Was a Beatle Baptized Catholic? Get Back
   to Where You Once Belonged! 81

Light of the World, Life of the Party 88

What's in a Name? 95

Are You Ready for Your Exit Interview? 101

About the Author 107

Introduction

Over the years, I've loved learning about the Catholic Church and its rich and sometimes startling 2000-year history. I discovered countless things I had never known and more than a few things I *thought* I knew but was wrong about. The more I studied, the more my correct understanding of things was reinforced and areas I was ignorant of (or misunderstood) were filled in and corrected. We can all benefit from that kind of learning, right?

Back in 1996, I launched a monthly, full-color Catholic journal called *Envoy Magazine* in an effort to help Catholics become more knowledgeable about the Bible, Church teachings, history, the saints, and so on. Thankfully, it was successful, and I published it for about 15 years. One of the departments I most enjoyed editing and collaborating on was the one-page quiz whimsically titled "InQUIZition." The subtitle was "wrack your brain and stretch your knowledge," a tongue-in-cheek play on words. Some of the quizzes in *this* book are adapted and greatly expanded from that popular department, and I hope that you enjoy reading these fun and fact-filled quizzes every bit as much as *Envoy* readers enjoyed the earlier ones. I wish to express a word of gratitude to the late Charlie Harvey, my son Timothy Madrid, and many others who suggested great ideas and collaborated with me in writing them. I also am deeply grateful to my Relevant Radio colleagues, especially Fr. Rocky, Richard Pieczynski, Colleen R. Schena, Elizabeth Groshek, and Emily Sturgeon for their tremendous skills, talents, and hard work in helping me bring this book to fruition.

The Catholic quizzes in this book are *much* more in-depth in terms of answers and explanations and, I hope, they'll be entertaining, informative, and valuable to you as you expand your storehouse of knowledge. In so doing, you'll also get to know Catholic history, teachings, customs, and notable personages more deeply, something of benefit for everyone, Catholic or not.

INQUIZITION

Much of the information in these pages is eminently practical. Like, for example, do you know what the Church's rule is on this issue? You should . . .
- a) Try to fast from food before Mass
- b) Fast from solid foods for an hour before Mass
- c) Fast from all food and liquids (except for water) for an hour before Mass
- d) Fast from all food and liquids (except for water) for an hour before Communion
- e) Fast from all food and liquids (no exception for water!) for an hour before Communion

If you guessed "d," you're correct, but it might surprise you how many Catholics, even devout, Mass-attending Catholics are a little fuzzy on this issue. (By the way, here's the relevant section from Code of Canon Law: "Can. 919 §1. A person who is to receive the Most Holy Eucharist is to abstain for at least one hour before holy communion from any food and drink, except for only water and medicine.")

The practical value of this quiz book is that it will not just inform you of a wide variety of facts about all things Catholic, it will also reinforce things you already know and "fill in the blanks" in areas about which you might not be well informed. And best of all, it's fun! So, whether you'd consider yourself a beginner, or intermediate in your knowledge, or even advanced, there's plenty here for you to learn and benefit from.

If you are a current Relevant Radio listener, this book is, in part, a thank you to you for your generous support. If you are not yet, I hope this book inspires you to want to tune in! And most of all, I pray it will help you live your Catholic Faith more joyfully, share it more gracefully, and (when necessary) defend it more charitably because, as the saying goes, "you can't give what you don't have." So, turn the page and enjoy a whole lot more to know and share.

Patrick Madrid, Summer 2022

Adventures in Theodicy

The Catholic Church has spent the last 2,000 years teaching the gospel of Jesus Christ, which gives us a clear doctrinal and moral path—even despite lots of disagreement and opposition. See if you can tell apart the good, the bad, and the downright heretical.

1. The three key elements of determining the morality or immorality of a human act are:
    a. serious matter, sufficient reflection, and deliberate consent
    b. the kingdom, the power, and the glory
    c. "In essentials unity, in non-essentials liberty, in all things charity" (St. Augustine)
    d. the object of the act, the circumstances, and the intention
    e. Does it feel good? Is anybody watching? Are you absolutely sure you won't get caught?

2. In Catholic parlance, what does the Latin word *peritus* mean?
    a. a parrot
    b. a little dog, like the one that held a torch for St. Dominic
    c. an expert theologian who assists a bishop, for example, at an ecumenical council
    d. a blind man (i.e., a blind guide who leads others astray, like in Matthew 15:14)
    e. a young patriarch (under 30 years of age)

INQUIZITION

3. What is the term for something that is made up of both good and evil?
    a. abulia
    b. agathokakological
    c. that last one is definitely not a real word
    d. Verisimilitude
    e. Cringe

4. According to tradition, what was the name of the Roman soldier who pierced the side of Christ on the Cross with a spear?
    a. Spiro (like Spiro Agnew)
    b. Cornelius
    c. Lance
    d. Septimus
    e. Longinus

5. Which is the most theologically accurate answer to the question: "What does it mean that Jesus Christ is 'true God and true man'?"
    a. He is 100% God but in the form of a perfect man, similar to how angels sometimes appear in human form.
    b. He is a highly exalted human person with many important attributes of God and is in-dwelled by God.
    c. He is 50% divine and 50% human.
    d. He is a 100% divine person and 100% human person with a divine and a human nature.
    e. He is a divine person with a divine nature and a human nature.

6. This early Church document is a summary of the teachings of the Twelve Apostles dating back to the early second century:
    a. the Shepherd of Hermas
    b. the Apostle's Creed
    c. the Didache

d. the collected epistles of St. Ignatius of Antioch
e. there is no such document dating back to the 1st or 2nd century

7. The First Vatican Council taught that the pope is infallible when, for example, he formally defines a dogma:
   a. *ex corde*
   b. *ex opera operato*
   c. *ex cathedra*
   d. *extramadura*
   e. *ex post facto*

8. According to Catholic moral theology the "principle of double effect"...
   a. requires that at least two morally good results must occur in order to outweigh doing something sinful to achieve a good end
   b. was condemned as a Protestant heresy by the Council of Trent
   c. means that you can never do something sinful unless you have two (or more) good reasons for doing so
   d. means that every sin has two negative effects: damage done to the sinner's soul and damage done to the Mystical Body of Christ (i.e., the Church)
   e. means (for example) that lethal force, when used in self-defense, can be morally permissible if the death of the aggressor is an unintended side-effect

9. What trait did every single pope between (but not including) Pope Adrian VI & Pope St. John Paul II have in common?
   a. they all died as martyrs
   b. their pontificates all lasted at least 5 years
   c. all were Italian

d. all wrote at least one papal encyclical
e. All were known to eat tacos occasionally

10. In his landmark 1993 encyclical on the nature, power, and beauty of truth, *Veritatis Splendor,* Pope St. John Paul II asserts the principle that some acts (like abortion) are "intrinsically evil." This means that:
    a. it's only really evil if nothing good comes from it
    b. it's always evil, except in certain circumstances
    c. it's always evil in itself and is never permitted under any circumstances or for any reason
    d. it's only really evil if you think it is. If you disagree, it can be morally okay for you.
    e. Whatever. He was just a white, male, European puppet of the patriarchy, so who cares.

11. What is "*Theodicy*"?
    a. An epic poem I wrote when I was in high school
    b. the solution to the apparent contradiction of how the existence of evil is compatible with an all-loving and all-powerful God
    c. the thesis presentation everyone in minor seminary gives before continuing to major seminary
    d. a Greek term for one who gives up everything to become a "fool for God"
    e. a derogatory term for a radio host with little or no theological knowledge

12. According to Catholic moral teaching, which of these activities (alone or with others) is intrinsically evil?
    a. depilation
    b. formication
    c. artificial breath control

    d. getting high on life
    e. none of the above

Answer Key

1. D. In layman's terms, ask yourself: What are you doing? What's the context in which you're doing it? And why are you doing it?

2. C. Literally one "skilled" in theology, Scripture, the Church Fathers, morals, etc. A notable example of a *peritus* at Vatican II was Fr. Joseph Ratzinger, who later was elected Pope Benedict XVI.

3. B. Seriously. That's a real word. You'll likely never hear me use it on the show, though.

4. E. The *Catholic Encyclopedia* says that a "famous Syriac manuscript of the Laurentian Library at Florence, illuminated by one Rabulas in the year 586" includes the name in Greek as a speculated denotation of the soldier as he pierces the side of Jesus. In that same sixth-century tradition, Longinus was both healed and converted from a drop of the Precious Blood (Robert Appleton Company, 1910, vol. 8, p. 773.)

5. E. The first two of the first four incorrect choices are *versions* of early Christological heresies (a) Monophysitism and (b) Nestorianism. The orthodox Catholic teaching is: "The unique and altogether singular event of the Incarnation of the Son of God does not mean that Jesus Christ is part God and part man, nor does it imply that He is the result of a confused mixture of the divine and the human. He became truly man while remaining truly God. Jesus Christ is true God and true man. During the first centuries, the Church had to defend and clarify this truth of faith against the heresies that falsified it" (CCC 464).

6. C. "Doctrine of the Twelve Apostles"— "A short treatise which

was accounted by some of the Fathers as next to Holy Scripture. It was rediscovered in 1873 . . . the contents may be divided into three parts: the first is the "Two Ways," the Way of Life and the Way of Death; the second part is a *rituale* dealing with baptism, fasting, and Holy Communion; the third speaks of the ministry. Doctrinal teaching is presupposed, and none is imparted" (*Catholic Encyclopedia*, vol. IV, p. 779).

7. C. Latin: "From the Chair." "Faithfully adhering to the tradition received from the beginning of the [C]hristian faith . . . with the approval of the Sacred Council, we teach and define as a divinely revealed dogma that when the Roman Pontiff speaks *ex cathedra*, that is, when, in the exercise of his office as shepherd and teacher of all Christians, in virtue of his supreme apostolic authority, he defines a doctrine concerning faith or morals to be held by the whole Church, he possesses, by the divine assistance promised to him in blessed Peter, that infallibility which the divine Redeemer willed his Church to enjoy in defining doctrine concerning faith or morals. Therefore, such definitions of the Roman Pontiff are of themselves, and not by the consent of the Church, irreformable" (*Pastor Aeternus*, 9). You'll find a great deal more about papal infallibility in my book, *Pope Fiction: Answers to 30 Myths and Misconceptions about the Papacy* (Basilica Press/St. Benedict Press, 2016).

8. E. "Double Effect" means, in principle, that if something that is not in itself intrinsically evil is done with an intended good goal (i.e. saving a life) but has a negative *unintended* consequence (i.e. the death of another), it is still morally permissible. For example, the *Catechism* teaches that "[t]he legitimate defense of persons and societies is not an exception to the prohibition against the murder of the innocent that constitutes intentional killing. 'The act of self-defense can have a double effect: the preservation of one's own life; and the killing of the aggressor. . . . The one is in-

tended, the other is not' (2263)."

9. C. True story! Between Pope Adrian VI (1459-1523, born in the Netherlands) and Pope St. John Paul II (1920-2005, born in Poland), every single pope was Italian. Bonus item for your good-to-know file: Pope Adrian VI was the only pope for the last 500 years (except for Pope Marcellus II, 1501-1555) to keep his own name when he became pope. All other popes assume a new name upon accepting their election.

10. C. Pope John Paul rightly reminds us that "negative moral precepts, [i.e.,] those prohibiting certain concrete actions or kinds of behavior as intrinsically evil, *do not allow for any legitimate exception. They do not leave room, in any morally acceptable way, for the 'creativity' of any contrary determination whatsoever*. Once the moral species of an action prohibited by a universal rule is concretely recognized, the only morally good act is that of obeying the moral law and of refraining from the action which it forbids" (*Veritatis Splendor*, 67).

11. B. See Peter Kreeft and Ronald Tacelli, S.J., *Handbook of Catholic Apologetics* (San Francisco: Ignatius Press, 2009, pp. 129-154).

12. E. Read the words again slowly! Merriam-Webster Dictionary defines *formication* as "an abnormal sensation resembling that made by insects [like ants] creeping in or on the skin."

It's All Greek (or Latin, or Aramaic) to Me

Let's put your language skills to the test. See if you could get by in Israel... in the days of Jesus and Mary!

1. The Hebrew biblical name *Ichabod* means:
    a. Icky body
    b. Headless body
    c. Where is the glory?
    d. Where is the love?
    e. What were you thinking?

2. Often used by St. Paul, what does the Greek word *koinonía* mean?
    a. love
    b. blessing
    c. hope
    d. communion
    e. faith

3. This biblical word refers to a deep and abiding conversion of the heart:
    a. *parousia*
    b. *katharos*
    c. *gyros*
    d. *kairos*
    e. *metánoia*

4. The biblical Greek word *kenosis* means:
    a. anointing
    b. blessing
    c. filling up
    d. perseverance
    e. emptying out

5. In Hebrew, the word *manna* means:
    a. heavenly dew
    b. meal ready to eat
    c. What is it?
    d. just in time
    e. God provides

6. What was Jesus' native language?
    a. Hebrew
    b. Aramaic
    c. Arabic
    d. Greek
    e. Chaldean

7. The Hebrew word *Golgotha* means:
    a. judgment seat
    b. place of the skull
    c. abandon all hope
    d. victory over death
    e. place of execution

8. The word *apostle* means:
    a. twelve
    b. chosen
    c. sent
    d. leader

e. remnant

9. In Hebrew, the word *Bethlehem* means:
    a. City of David
    b. Home of Shepherds
    c. Star of Wonder
    d. House of Bread
    e. Prince of Peace

10. The name *Michael* means:
    a. God is in charge!
    b. Sword of God
    c. Who is like unto God?
    d. Who can stand before God?
    e. Mighty warrior

11. The name *Gabriel* means:
    a. God is my strength
    b. Beloved of God
    c. Child of God
    d. Servant of God
    e. Who is like unto God?

12. The Greek word *baptizein*, from which we get the word "baptize," means:
    a. to make clean
    b. pool of water
    c. to dip or immerse
    d. born again
    e. Holy Ghost power

Answer Key

1. C. Hebrew אִי־כָבוֹד (*I-kabod*) = "There is no glory." Poor kid. Can you imagine? "Then she named the child Ichabod, saying, 'The glory has departed from Israel!' because the ark of God had been captured" (1 Sam. 4:21).

2. D. Κοινωνία (*koinonía*) = fellowship, communion, sharing (see Acts 2:42, 1 Corinthians 1:9, 1 Corinthians 10:16, Philippians 2:1, etc.).

3. E. Greek: μετάνοια (*metánoia*) = change of mind, repentance (*Strong's* 3341) See Matthew 3:8-11, Luke 24:47, Romans 2:4).

4. E. Greek: κενόω (*kenoó* — pronounced "ken-ah-oh") = to empty. Philippians 2:6-11 (borrowing from Isaiah 52 and 53) is a particularly important passage with deep Christological meaning where it says that Jesus Christ "was in the form of God, did not count equality with God a thing to be grasped, but *emptied* himself, taking the form of a servant, being born in the likeness of men. And being found in human form he humbled himself and became obedient unto death, even death on a cross. Therefore God has highly exalted him and bestowed on him the name which is above every name, that at the name of Jesus every knee should bow, in heaven and on earth and under the earth, and every tongue confess that Jesus Christ is Lord, to the glory of God the Father."

5. C. A bread-like substance that God provided as food for the Israelites as they wandered for 40 years in the desert (Exodus 16; Numbers 11:6-9) that foreshadowed and symbolized the Holy Eucharist. "Jesus answered them, 'This is the work of God, that you believe in him whom he has sent.' So they said to him, 'Then what sign do you do, that we may see, and believe you? What work do you perform? Our fathers ate the manna in the wilder-

ness; as it is written, "He gave them bread from heaven to eat."' Jesus then said to them, 'Truly, truly, I say to you, it was not Moses who gave you the bread from heaven; my Father gives you the true bread from heaven. For the bread of God is that which comes down from heaven, and gives life to the world.' They said to him, 'Lord, give us this bread always.' Jesus said to them, 'I am the bread of life; he who comes to me shall not hunger, and he who believes in me shall never thirst'" (John 6:29-35).

6. B. Aramaic was the day-to-day language spoken by Jews in the land of Israel at that time, the language that developed because of the Babylonian captivity (see 1 Kings 12 & 17, 2 Kings 17, Nehemiah 8 & 9). Hebrew was primarily the language of Scripture and Jesus was fluent in it (see Luke 4:17-21). Greek, which Jesus very likely spoke as well, was extremely widespread across the Mediterranean basin as the primary language of commerce and diplomacy, especially in Egypt and the lands east of Rome.

7. B. See Matthew 27:3, Mark 15:22, and John 19:17.

8. C. In Greek, ἀπόστολος (*apóstolos*) = "messenger, he that is sent" (*Strong's* 649). Countless volumes have been written about the Apostles (for example, Pope Benedict XVI's excellent *The Apostles*, Ignatius Press, 2015), but for the purposes of this question, the Twelve Apostles, the Lord's closest collaborators and inner circle, were *sent* by Jesus to "go into the whole world, making disciples of all nations" (Matthew 28:19-20).

9. D. The significance of the name of the little town where Jesus was born cannot be underestimated. The "house of bread" motif is one of the fulfilments of prophecy concerning the coming Messiah: "But you, O Bethlehem Ephrathah, who are little to be among the clans of Judah, from you shall come forth for me one who is to be ruler in Israel, whose origin is from of old, from ancient days" (Micah 5:2). It also signifies how Christ, particularly

in the Holy Eucharist, is the fulfillment of the miraculous bread from heaven, the manna in the desert (Exodus 16) with which God fed the Israelites for a time as they wandered. Jesus said, "For the bread of God is that which comes down from heaven and gives life to the world" and "I am the bread of life; he who comes to me shall not hunger, and he who believes in me shall never thirst" (John 6:33, 35).

10. C. The Greek Μιχαήλ (*michaēl*) is a transliteration of the Hebrew מִיכָאֵל (*mîkā'ēl*) "who is like God?" He is a prominent angel and may be seraphim rather than archangel (some Church Fathers posit this). In any case, divine revelation does not tell us that one way or the other. The Archangel Michael appears in Daniel 10:13,21, 12:1, Jude 9, and Revelation 12:7. From these, we give Saint Michael four "offices": "1) To fight against Satan. 2) To rescue the souls of the faithful from the power of the enemy, especially at the hour of death. 3) To be the champion of God's people, the Jews in the Old Law, the Christians in the New Testament...and 4) To call away from earth and bring men's souls to judgment" ("Michael," *Catholic Encyclopedia*, vol. 10, p. 276).

11. A. Gabriel (Hebrew: גַּבְרִיאֵל (*gaḇrî'ēl*) = the "Hero of God" or the "Strong Man of God"). Only four appearances of Gabriel are recorded: Daniel 8, Daniel 9, the annunciation of John the Baptist's birth to Zechariah (Luke 1:5-25) and Jesus' birth to Mary (Luke 1:26-38). He is the "angel of mercy" to Michael's "angel of judgment" ("Gabriel," *Catholic Encyclopedia*, vol. 6, p. 330).

12. C. The Catholic Church teaches that both baptism by infusion (pouring) and immersion are valid, even though immersion was much more commonly practiced in the early Church. See Patrick Madrid, *Why Is That in Tradition?* (Our Sunday Visitor, Huntington, IN).

Somebody Call a (Church) Doctor!

The most recent saint to be officially named a Doctor of the Church (this year), brings the total of brilliant men and women, scholars and mystics, up to 37. Can you name them all?

1. He miraculously cured a boy who was choking on a fishbone:
    a. St. Peter
    b. St. Blaise
    c. St. James the Greater
    d. St. Francis of Assisi
    e. St. Bede

2. Which saint is known as the "Seraphic Doctor" and was the subject of much of Pope Benedict XVI's theological studies?
    a. St. Albert the Great
    b. St. Thomas Aquinas
    c. St. Bonaventure
    d. St. Seraphim Medicus
    e. St. Augustine of Hippo

3. Who of the following has not been named a Doctor of the Church?
    a. St. Teresa of Avilà
    b. St. Philip Neri
    c. St. Anthony of Padua
    d. St. Thomas Aquinas
    e. St. Hildegard of Bingen

SOMEBODY CALL A (CHURCH) DOCTOR!

4. This is most quoted Doctor of the Church in the *Catechism of the Catholic Church*:
    a. St. Thomas
    b. St. Ambrose
    c. St. Bonaventure
    d. St. Augustine
    e. St. Bede

5. He is called the "Father of Scholasticism":
    a. St. Anselm
    b. St. Peter Damian
    c. St. Albert the Great
    d. St. Thomas Aquinas
    e. St. Bonaventure

6. This Saint is known as the Doctor Marianus because of his many writings on the Blessed Virgin Mary:
    a. St. Thomas Aquinas
    b. Drew Mariani
    c. St. Bernard of Clairvaux
    d. St. Anselm of Canterbury
    e. St. Albert the Great

7. Who is known as "The Doctor of Grace"?
    a. St. Augustine
    b. St. Cyril of Jerusalem
    c. St. Justin Martyr
    d. St. Bonaventure
    e. Bootsy Collins (Just kidding. Though he is widely regarded as a doctor of funk)

8. Falling asleep during a boring sermon is a time-honored Catholic custom. This lad fell asleep during a sermon delivered by St. Paul himself!
    a. Silas
    b. Barnabas
    c. Drowsyus
    d. Alexander the Coppersmith
    e. Eutychus

9. A "Red Mass" is a special Mass celebrated for:
    a. Courts, judges, and lawyers
    b. Doctors and physicians
    c. Patients
    d. Prisoners and the conversion of sinners
    e. Radio hosts

10. Which of these is properly called a "human act"?
    a. sneezing in a crowded elevator
    b. belching accidentally after a particularly satisfying meal
    c. when someone irritating rubs you the wrong way
    d. deciding whether to attend Mass on Sunday or stay home and sleep in
    e. none of the above

11. Who among the following has been formally declared a Doctor of the Church?
    a. St. Pius IX
    b. Pius XII
    c. St. Luke the Physician
    d. St. Clare of Assisi
    e. St. Thérèse of Lisieux

SOMEBODY CALL A (CHURCH) DOCTOR!

12. Which sin does St. Thomas Aquinas identify as one of the most dangerous, if not *the* most dangerous?
    a. despair
    b. lust
    c. disbelief
    d. neglecting to listen regularly to *The Patrick Madrid Show*
    e. tampering with liturgical rubrics

Answer Key

1. B. Born in Sebaste, Armenia (now by Sivas, modern-day Turkey), he was a holy bishop who was martyred in 316 after being tortured for Christ and then beheaded.

2. C. "Doctor of the Church, Cardinal-Bishop of Albano, Minister General of the Friars Minor, born near Viterbo in 1221; died at Lyons, July 15, 1274" (*Catholic Encyclopedia*, vol. II, pp. 648-649). "The title by which St. Bonaventure is most readily known was given him while he was still alive. His thought is entwined with love; it quickly springs to seraphic or angelic heights. As a teacher, he gives expression to the life of the Seraphic Saint, St. Francis of Assisi" (*The 33 Doctors of the Church*, p. 356).

3. B. Born in Florence (1515), died in Rome (1595), canonized in 1622.

4. D. St. Augustine had countless profound theological insights and keen arguments, many of which are still drawn upon by theologians today alongside St. Thomas Aquinas; Aquinas himself even quotes Augustine countless times in his extensive *Summa Theologiae*.

5. A. (1033-1109), St. Anselm of Canterbury was born into a wealthy noble family in Aosta, Italy, but eventually entered a

monastery in Normandy, France, when he was 27. He became the Archbishop of Canterbury, England, in 1093. "His active work as a pastor and stalwart champion of the Church makes Anselm one of the chief figures in religious history. The sweet influence of his spiritual teaching was felt far and wide, and its fruits were seen in many lands. His stand for the freedom of the Church in a crisis of medieval history had far-reaching effects long after his own time. As a writer and a thinker he may claim yet higher rank, and his influence on the course of philosophy and Catholic theology was even deeper and more enduring. If he stands on the one hand with Gregory VII, and Innocent III, and Thomas Becket; on the other he may claim a place beside Athanasius, Augustine, and Thomas Aquinas.... [He was] declared a Doctor of the Church by Pope Clement XI, 1720, and in the office read on his feast day (April 21) it is said that his works are a pattern for all theologians" ("Anselm," *Catholic Encyclopedia*, vol. I, pp. 548-549).

6. D. Surprise! St. Anselm of Canterbury was a busy man.

7. A. St. Augustine is called the "Doctor of Grace" due to his constant and intelligent combatting of heresies, especially the Pelagian heresy, which denied the existence of Original Sin as well as grace, also insisting that life was lived wholly dependent on human free will. This Doctor "made a very strong case for grace and man's complete dependence upon it. In doing this he grappled with problems connected with man's nature—Original Sin, infant baptism, and predestination. He is the great pioneer in this most difficult field, although the common teaching of the Church is more moderate than his system" (*The 33 Doctors of the Church*, Fr. Christopher Rengers, O.F.M., Cap. [TAN Books, 2010, p. 124).

8. E. As a radio host, I find this biblical incident to be a good reminder to not go on too long with my comments! "On the first

day of the week, when we were gathered together to break bread, Paul talked with them, intending to depart on the morrow; and he prolonged his speech until midnight. There were many lights in the upper chamber where we were gathered. And a young man named Eutychus was sitting in the window. He sank into a deep sleep as Paul talked still longer; and being overcome by sleep, he fell down from the third story and was taken up dead" (Acts 20:7-9). (Don't worry, he was revived by Paul just a verse later!)

9. A. "Catholic Lawyer Guilds throughout the world, in conjunction with their bishops, sponsor a Red Mass annually in order to invoke divine guidance and strength during the coming term of the Court. It is celebrated in honor of the Holy Spirit as the source of wisdom, understanding, counsel, and fortitude, gifts that shine forth preeminently in the dispensing of justice in the courtroom as well as in the individual lawyer's office. It also offers prayers for all men and women in the legal profession, judiciary, and public life, asking that they be blessed with wisdom and understanding." These special Masses began in Paris, 1245, and the first one States-side was in New York City on October 6, 1928. The Basilica of the National Shrine of the Immaculate Conception in D. C. has attendees at their Red Masses from Congress, the Supreme Court, and even presidents. ("History of the Red Mass," Catholic Bar Association, catholicbar.org).

10. D. An act is deemed a "human act" if it is intentional and results from a deliberate act of your will, i.e, you *choose* to do or not do something that in itself has a moral quality. The act can be morally good, bad, or neutral and is expressed either internally in the mind (e.g., envy, pride, wrath) or externally through a bodily action (e.g., sexual sin, stealing, punching someone in the face).

11. E. Pope John Paul II: "Thérèse of Lisieux is a young person. She reached the maturity of holiness in the prime of youth. As such,

she appears as a Teacher of evangelical life, particularly effective in illumining the paths of young people, who must be the leaders and witnesses of the Gospel to the new generations. Thérèse of the Child Jesus is not only the youngest Doctor of the Church, but is also the closest to us in time, as if to emphasize the continuity with which the Spirit of the Lord sends His messengers to the Church, men and women as teachers and witnesses to the faith.... [She] is a Teacher for our time, which thirsts for living and essential words, for heroic and credible acts of witness" (*Divini Amoris Scientia,* October 19, 1997).

12. A. "Unbelief is due to a man not believing God's own truth; while the hatred of God arises from man's will being opposed to God's goodness itself; whereas despair consists in a man ceasing to hope for a share of God's goodness. Hence it is clear that unbelief and hatred of God are against God as He is in Himself, while despair is against Him, according as His good is partaken of by us. Wherefore strictly speaking it is more grievous sin to disbelieve God's truth, or to hate God, than not to hope to receive glory from Him.... If, however, despair be compared to the other two sins from our point of view, then despair is more dangerous, since hope withdraws us from evils and induces us to seek for good things, so that when hope is given up, men rush headlong into sin, and are drawn away from good works" (*Summa Theologiae*, II IIae, q. 20, a. 3).

Is It Cheating if You Use Your Bible?

The Bible contains 73 books: 46 in the Old Testament, 27 in the New Testament, over three millennia's worth of divine revelation, and a 99.99% chance you can find many of the answers to these questions in its pages.

1. "Synoptic" as in "synoptic Gospel" means:
    a. written without error
    b. with a pure heart
    c. grammatically correct
    d. looks good (i.e., favorable optics)
    e. seen with one eye

2. What did the "man" with whom Jacob wrestles say to him?
    a. "Let me go, for the day is breaking."
    b. "I give up!"
    c. "Had enough?"
    d. "Did you letter in this or *what*?"
    e. "Uncle!"

3. Who said, "Charity covers a multitude of sins"?
    a. St. Peter
    b. St. Paul
    c. St. James
    d. St. Jude
    e. Jesus

4. What does the name "Jesus" mean in Hebrew?
    a. Messiah
    b. God Is with Us

c. House of Bread
d. The Lord Is Salvation
e. Prince of Peace

5. According to the Gospel account, what did the woman who was about to be stoned for being caught committing adultery cry out?
    a. "Stop, in the name of love, before you break my heart!"
    b. "I shot the sheriff, but I did not shoot the deputy."
    c. Nothing.
    d. "Lord, help me!"
    e. "Rock me gently, rock me slowly"

6. How many times does the word "antichrist" appear in the Book of Revelation?
    a. 666
    b. 2
    c. 3
    d. 7
    e. 0

7. This Old Testament personage had a talking donkey!
    a. Amos
    b. Balaam
    c. Jeremiah
    d. Shrekiah
    e. Elias

8. Derives from the Greek word meaning "slanderer":
    a. apostate
    b. devil
    c. heretic
    d. demon
    e. tabloid

9. At the Council of Jerusalem, the Apostles settled a dispute by agreeing that
    a. circumcision and following kosher food laws are not necessary to be Christian
    b. circumcision is only necessary for men who really want to prove their love for God
    c. Christians are obliged to eat fish on Fridays
    d. Taco Tuesdays would henceforth be informally observed by the universal Church as a minor feast day dedicated giving thanks to the Lord for His many blessings
    e. St. Peter was the first pope

10. The biblical teaching that "a man is justified by his works and *not* by faith alone" appears in which New Testament epistle?
    a. 1 Peter
    b. 2 Timothy
    c. James
    d. Hebrews
    e. Jude

11. The "behemoth" (beh-HEE-muth) mentioned in the Book of Job was a/an
    a. Balrog of Morgoth
    b. brontosaurus
    c. hippopotamus
    d. whale
    e. elephant

12. The Hebrew name *Deborah* means:
    a. beautiful smile
    b. bee
    c. covenant

d. the cattle are dying
e. of Borah

Answer Key

1. E. Matthew, Mark, and Luke are known as the synoptic Gospels. The term "is derived from the fact that these Gospels admit, differently from the evangelical narrative of St. John, of being arranged and harmonized section by section, so as to allow the eye to realize at a glance (synopsis) the numerous passages which are common to them, and also the portions which are peculiar either to only two, or even to only one, of them" (*Catholic Encyclopedia*, vol. XIV, p. 389-390).

2. A. He appeared in the form of a man, but was actually an angel. See Genesis 32:24-32 for the whole sweaty story.

3. A. See 1 Peter 4:8.

4. D. "*Yehoshua*" translated into English as Joshua (OT) and Jesus (NT). *Catholic Encyclopedia* says, "The word Jesus is the Latin form of the Greek Ἰησοῦς (*Iesous*), which in turn is the transliteration of the Hebrew *Jeshua*, or *Joshua*, or again *Jehoshua*, meaning "[God] is salvation." Though the name in one form or another occurs frequently in the Old Testament, it was not borne by a person of prominence between the time of Joshua, the son of Nun and Joshua, the high priest in the days of Zorobabel. It was also the name of the author of Ecclesiasticus, of one of Christ's ancestors mentioned in the genealogy, found in the Third Gospel (Luke 3:29), and one of the St. Paul's companions (Colossians 4:11) .... The Greek name is connected with verb ἰάομαι (*iasthai*), 'to heal'; it is therefore, not surprising that some of the Greek Fathers allied the word Jesus with [the] same root . . . Though about the time of Christ the name Jesus appears to have been fairly com-

mon (see Josephus, *Jewish Antiquities*, 15:9:2, 17:8:1; 20:9:1) it was imposed on our Lord by God's express order (Luke 1:31; Matthew 1:21), to [show] that the Child was destined to 'save his people from their sins'" (vol. 8, p. 374).

5. C. See John 8:1-11.

6. E. That's right. Not even once.

7. B. See Numbers 22 for this remarkable story.

8. B. Greek: διάβολος (*diabolos*) = "slanderous, accusing falsely." The word appears 38 times in the Greek New Testament, sometimes referring to the Evil One (see Luke 4:1-13), other times referring to malicious behavior among human beings (see 1 Timothy 3:11, Titus 2:3).

9. A. See Acts 10 for how God revealed to St. Peter that Jesus Christ's inauguration of the New Covenant had fulfilled all of the requirements of the Law of Moses, thereby making the Mosaic ceremonial laws (e.g., not eating pork, kosher food laws, circumcision, etc.) no longer binding on Christians. See Acts 15 for how the Apostles, after hearing Saint Peter explain this divine revelation, were guided by the Holy Spirit to affirm this truth for the whole Church. (*P.S.* Although it is a custom from ancient times to abstain from meat on Fridays throughout the year as an act of penitential mortification, it has *never* been obligatory for Catholics to eat fish on Fridays (or any day of the year!). That's just an urban legend.)

10. C. "You see that a man is justified by works and not by faith alone…For as the body apart from the spirit is dead, so faith apart from works is dead" (James 2:24, 26).

11. C. "Generally translated by 'great beasts,' [behemoth] in its wider signification it includes all mammals living on earth, but in the stricter sense is applied to domesticated quadrupeds at large.

However in Job 40:10, where it is left untranslated and considered as a proper name, it indicates a particular animal. The description of this animal has long puzzled the commentators. Many of them now admit that it represents the hippopotamus, so well known to the ancient Egyptians; it might possibly correspond as well to the rhinoceros" ("Animals in the Bible," *Catholic Encyclopedia*, vol. 1, p. 519).

12. B. A biblical judge and a prophetess. "She used to sit under the palm of Deborah between Ramah and Bethel in the hill country of Ephraim; and the people of Israel came up to her for judgment" (see Judges 4 & 5).

State of the Hypostatic Union

Our Catholic Faith's doctrines are rooted deep in Scripture and Apostolic Tradition. And nothing spurred action from the Church's Magisterium like the popularization of a heresy. Let's see how well you know the Church's ecumenical councils and the heresies that necessitated them.

1. The "hypostatic union" refers to the unique union, in Jesus Christ, of the following:
    a. two persons in one nature
    b. two wills in one mind
    c. two wills in one nature
    d. two natures in one person
    e. two persons in one body

2. This heresy held that the Second Person of the Trinity, the Logos, "took the place of" the spiritual part of Jesus' soul, rendering Christ's humanity incomplete:
    a. Arianism
    b. Antinomianism
    c. Apollinarianism
    d. Docetism
    e. Totalitarianism

3. The council of Chalcedon (451 A.D.) condemned this heresy:
    a. Arianism
    b. Montanism
    c. Monophysitism
    d. Monotheletism
    e. Modernism

4. What early heresy denied the true divinity of Christ?
    a. Sabellianism
    b. Arianism
    c. Nestorianism
    d. Patripassianism
    e. Pelagianism

5. How many sessions did the Council of Trent have (1545-63)?
    a. 1
    b. 7
    c. 12
    d. 20
    e. 25

6. Which of these pre-Revolutionary American Colonies was early on considered a safe refuge for English Catholics fleeing persecution by Protestants?
    a. Connecticut
    b. Vermont
    c. Virginia
    d. Maryland
    e. Maine

7. Which Greek or Latin title refers specifically to Mary's role as the Mother of God?
    a. *Huperdulía*
    b. *Sedes Sapientiae*
    c. *Mater Dolorosa*
    d. *Theotókos*
    e. *Regina Caeli*

8. Which early Church Council defined the dogma of the hypostatic union of Jesus Christ (true God and true man) and proclaimed the Marian title of *Theotókos*?
    a. Nicaea (A.D. [CS3] 325)
    b. Constantinople (A.D. 381)
    c. Ephesus (A.D. 431)
    d. Chalcedon (A.D. 451)
    e. Constantinople II (A.D. 553)

9. At which general Church Council was the Arian heresy first formally condemned?
    a. Nicaea I
    b. Nicaea II
    c. Constantinople I
    d. Chalcedon
    e. Ephesus

10. In what year did the Council of Chalcedon convene?
    a. 325
    b. 389
    c. 431
    d. 451
    e. 553

11. According to the Vatican II document *Sacrosanctum Concilium*, what form of liturgical music should have "pride of place" at Mass?
    a. pipe organ
    b. acoustic guitars
    c. soft rock
    d. Gregorian chant
    e. Vatican II did not specify any particular form of liturgical music as having any special "pride of place"

12. How did Jesus address the Father in prayer?
    a. Lord
    b. Father God
    c. Yahweh
    d. El Shaddai
    e. Abba

Answer Key

1. D. *Catechism of the Catholic Church,* 461: "Taking up St. John's expression, 'The Word became flesh' (John 1:14), the Church calls [the] 'Incarnation' the fact that the Son of God assumed a human nature in order to accomplish our salvation in it. In a hymn cited by St. Paul, the Church sings the mystery of the Incarnation: 'Have this mind among yourselves, which is yours in Christ Jesus, who, though He was in the form of God, did not count equality with God a thing to be grasped, but emptied Himself, taking the form of a servant, being born in the likeness of men. And being found in human form He humbled Himself and became obedient unto death, even death on a cross' (Philippians 2:5-8)."

2. C. "A Christological theory, according to which Christ had a human body and a human sensitive soul, but no human rational mind, the Divine Logos taking the place of this last." In condemning this error, Pope Damasus I, in the Council of Rome, 381, pronounced "anathema against them who say that the Word of God is in the human flesh in lieu and place of the human rational and intellective soul. For, the Word of God is the Son Himself. Neither did He come in the flesh to replace, but rather to assume and preserve from sin and save the rational and intellective

soul of man" ("Apollinarianism," *Catholic Encyclopedia*, vol. I, p. 615).

3. C. The heresy that in Christ there is only one nature, a fusion between the divine and human natures. The *Catholic Encyclopedia* contrasts two heresies with the orthodox Catholic teaching: "*Monophysites*: One person, one hypostasis, one nature. *Nestorians*: One person, two hypostases, two natures. *Catholics*: One person, one hypostasis, two natures." [H]owever harmless the [Monophysite] formula 'one nature' might look at first sight, it led in fact immediately to serious and disastrous consequences.... [making it] impossible to avoid one of two conclusions, either that the whole Divine Nature became man and suffered and died, or else that each of the three Persons had a Divine Nature of His own" (vol. X, pp. 494-495).

4. B. Arius (256-336), a Catholic priest from Egypt, proposed the notion that Jesus had a nature similar to God's, but ultimately was not the same. Therefore, the son of God was a superhuman creature with many godlike qualities, but not true God. This heresy proved to be as virulent as it was hardy and lasted for centuries. First condemned by the Catholic Church at the 1st Council of Nicaea in A.D. 325, Arianism's denial of the divinity of Christ was far simpler and easier to grasp than the truth of the Triune God, Father, Son, and Holy Spirit. The orthodox Catholic correction of the Arian proposition of Jesus being "ὁμοιούσιος" (*homoioousios*, Greek: of *similar* or *like* substance of the Father) literally came down to one vowel: "i" – the Council promulgated the term "ὁμοούσιος" (*homoousios*, Greek of the *same substance*). Among the many Church Fathers who combated Arianism was the great St. Athanasius of Alexandria (circa 296-373) who engaged in vigorous apologetics for many years in defense of the divinity of Christ and the Trinity as defined by the First Council of Nicaea.

5. E. The Church's 19th ecumenical council (December 13, 1545 – December 4, 1563). "Its main object was the definitive determination of the doctrines of the Church in answer to the heresies of the Protestants; a further object was the execution of a thorough reform of the inner life of the Church by removing the numerous abuses that had developed in it" ("Council of Trent," *Catholic Encyclopedia*, vol XV, p. 30) [T]he council was strongly influenced by Saint Thomas. Pope Leo XIII said, "The ecumenical councils... have always been careful to hold Thomas Aquinas in singular honor.... *But the chief and special glory of Thomas, one which he has shared with none of the* [other] *Catholic Doctors, is that the Fathers of Trent made it part of the order of conclave to lay upon the altar, together with sacred Scripture and the decrees of the supreme Pontiffs, the Summa of Thomas Aquinas, whence to seek counsel, reason, and inspiration"* (*Aeterni Patris*, 22, 1879).

6. D. The first Mass was celebrated in Maryland on the feast of the Annunciation in 1634. Jesuit Father Andrew White, in "Narrative of the Voyage of The Ark and The Dove," wrote: "we celebrated Mass for the first time [on] the island.... This had never been done before in this part of the world." What started out as a handful of faithful laity and priests to establish a colony of the faith became one of foundational states in the United States. "The genial climate, the fertile soil, the liberal conditions of plantation promulgated by the lord proprietary, the security and safety enjoyed by the colonists, the religious freedom and equality secured to the members of every Christian denomination, soon attracted a numerous immigration, and the colony grew apace." ("Maryland," *Catholic Encyclopedia*, vol. IX, pp. 755-760).

7. D. Greek: Θεοτόκος = God bearer. Latin: *Dei Genitrix* or *Mater Dei* = mother of God. "This is the declaration of the correct faith proclaimed everywhere. This was the sentiment of the holy Fathers; therefore they ventured to call the Holy Virgin, the Mother

of God (*theotókos*), not as if the nature of the Word or his divinity had its beginning from the Holy Virgin, but because of her was born that holy body with a rational soul, to which the Word being personally united is said to be born according to the flesh" (Council of Ephesus, A.D. 431).

8. C. *Catechism of the Catholic Church,* 495: "Called in the Gospels 'the mother of Jesus,' Mary is acclaimed by Elizabeth, at the prompting of the Spirit and even before the birth of her son, as 'the mother of my Lord.' (Luke 1:43). In fact, the One whom she conceived as man by the Holy Spirit, who truly became her Son according to the flesh, was none other than the Father's eternal Son, the second person of the Holy Trinity. Hence the Church confesses that Mary is truly [the] 'Mother of God' (*Theotókos*)."

9. A. "[I]n the presence of our most religious Sovereign Constantine, investigation was made of matters concerning the impiety and transgression of Arius and his adherents; and it was unanimously decreed that he and his impious opinion should be anathematized, together with the blasphemous words and speculations in which he indulged, blaspheming the Son of God, and saying that he [Jesus] is from things that are not, and that before he was begotten he was not, and that there was a time when he was not, and that the Son of God is by his free will capable of vice and virtue; saying also that he is a creature. All these things the holy Synod has anathematized, not even enduring to hear his impious doctrine and madness and blasphemous words" ("First Council of Nicæa: A.D. 325, *Synodal Letter*" *Nicene and Post-Nicene Fathers, Second Series, vol. 14.*, p.53).

10. D. The primary goal of the fourth ecumenical council, held in the fall of A.D. 451 in what is now a district of the city of Constantinople, "was to assert the orthodox Catholic doctrine against the heresy of Eutyches [Arianism] and the Monophysites, al-

though ecclesiastical discipline and jurisdiction also occupied the council's attention" ("Chalcedon," *Catholic Encyclopedia*, vol. III, p. 555).

11. D. "The Church acknowledges Gregorian chant as specially suited to the Roman liturgy: therefore, other things being equal, it should be given pride of place in liturgical services. But other kinds of sacred music, especially polyphony, are by no means excluded from liturgical celebrations, so long as they accord with the spirit of the liturgical action" (*Documents of Vatican II*, "*Sacrosanctum Concilium*," 116).

12. E. From Aramaic, rendered in Greek as Ἀββᾶ (Abba = father) "a customary title of God in prayer, whenever it occurs in the N.T., see Mark 14:36; Romans 8:15; Galatians 4:6" (*Thayer's Greek Lexicon*, p. 1).

Very Clever! You Got Me Monologuing!

The Bible is filled with profound soliloquies, inspirational songs, dramatic laments and classic one-liners. How well do you know these iconic words and the people who said them?

1. How many words spoken by St. Joseph are quoted in the New Testament?
    a. too many to count
    b. 12
    c. 33
    d. 7
    e. St. Joseph said words? Where?

2. Which Pharisee said of Christianity, "Let these men alone, for if this work be of men, it will fail. But if it be of God, you cannot overthrow it" (Acts 5:34)?
    a. Hillel
    b. Gamaliel
    c. Nicodemus
    d. Ananias
    e. Joseph of Arimathea

3. How many "smooth stones" does the Bible say young David brought to confront Goliath the mighty Philistine giant?
    a. two
    b. three
    c. five
    d. seven
    e. he only needed one, baby!

4. What early church did Jesus rebuke for being "neither hot nor cold, but lukewarm"?
    a. Laodicea
    b. Smyrna
    c. Ephesus
    d. Philadelphia
    e. Chicago

5. The Old Testament prophet Jonah was sent by God to warn which of these cities:
    a. Tyre
    b. Sidon
    c. Nineveh
    d. Sodom
    e. Jericho

6. Which of these animals is not mentioned in the Bible?
    a. dog
    b. house cat
    c. ape
    d. dromedary
    e. weasel

7. Which of these is *not* one of the Four Horsemen of the Apocalypse mentioned in Revelation 6?
    a. Conquest
    b. War
    c. Famine
    d. Death
    e. Earthquakes

8. What did Goliath the Philistine take with him to battle David?

a. the power of friendship (and a super soaker)
   b. spear and battle axe
   c. sword and spear
   d. bow staff skills
   e. An ancient form of nunchucks

9. Which New Testament letter contains the exhortation: "I found it necessary to write appealing to you to contend for the faith which was once for all delivered to the saints"?
   a. 1 Corinthians
   b. Galatians
   c. 2 John
   d. Ephesians
   e. Jude

10. In his numerous chapters of dialogue, who told Job to blame God for having caused his troubles?
    a. the devil
    b. Job's neighbors
    c. Job's children
    d. Job's wife
    e. Job's therapist

11. In Revelation 1:8 the Lord Jesus declares, "I am the Alpha and the…"
    a. Omicron
    b. Beta
    c. Zeta
    d. Delta
    e. Omega

12. Which book is second only to Isaiah in number of times quoted in the New Testament?

a. Psalms
b. Genesis
c. Exodus
d. Daniel
e. Obadiah

Answer Key

1. E. Interestingly, though the Gospels do not contain even a single direct quote from Saint Joseph, Matthew 1:25 offers the next best thing by saying of him that "*he called His name Jesus*" (Matthew 1:25).

2. B. Gamaliel was a wise man. And look! The Catholic Church still exists two thousand years later!

3. C. See 1 Samuel 17 for details of their dramatic showdown.

4. A. See Rev. 3:15, and Jesus follows it with, "because you are lukewarm, neither hot nor cold, I will spit you out of my mouth"!

5. C. This site is on the outskirts of the modern-day city of Mosul in northern Iraq.

6. B. Sorry, cats. This doesn't prove that all dogs go to heaven, of course (or cats for that matter), but it's interesting just how many animals are mentioned by name in the Bible ("Animals in the Bible," *Catholic Encyclopedia*, vol. I, pp. 517-526).

7. E.

8. C. See 1 Samuel 17:45-47 for his dramatic entry into battle: "You come against me with sword and spear and scimitar [a curved sword, from Persia], but I come against you in the name of the Lord of hosts…"

9. E. See Jude 1:3.

10. D. Talk about someone who needed to listen to *The Patrick Madrid Show* to get her mind right! Job's wife had the audacity to taunt him, saying, "Do you still hold fast your integrity? Curse God and die." *Whoa!* "But he said to her, 'You speak as one of the foolish women would speak. Shall we receive good at the hand of God, and shall we not receive evil?' In all this Job did not sin with his lips" — Right on! Way to stand tall and stay true to God in the midst of afflictions, brother! (Job 2:9-10).

11. E. *A* & *Ω*, the first and last letters of the Greek alphabet. This is an important passage demonstrating the divinity of Jesus (see verses 7-8) along with passages such as Revelation 1:17, 2:8, and 22:13 where Jesus declares that He is the "first and the last," "the alpha and the omega." Compare these with Isaiah 41:4 and 48:12 where God declares that He alone is "the first and the last." Jesus clearly proclaims His true divinity by invoking Himself these sacred titles for God.

12. A. The top ten Old Testament books most quoted in the New Testament are Isaiah (419), Psalms (414), Exodus (240), Genesis (238), Deuteronomy (196), Ezekiel (141), Daniel (133), Jeremiah (125), Leviticus (107), Numbers (73).

A Potpourri of Popery

After centuries of popes, it's a wonder that there are any names left for a new pontiff to choose from...

1. Which pope had a reputation for cracking jokes and telling humorous stories?
    a. Heaven forbid! No pope has had such a frivolous reputation.
    b. Pope John XXIII
    c. Pope Alexander VIII
    d. Pope Hilarius
    e. Saint Philip Neri

2. What is the *Pater Noster* commonly known as in English?
    a. the Rosary
    b. a blessing for fathers
    c. prayer to St. Joseph, Foster Father of Jesus
    d. the Our Father
    e. the Latin version of the "Faith of Our Fathers" hymn

3. Who was the first pope to be photographed while pope?
    a. Pope Leo XIII
    b. Pope Pius X
    c. Pope Pius IX
    d. Pope Pictorius I
    e. Pope Gregory XVI

4. The Greek phrase *Kyrie Eleison* means:
    a. amen and a woman

b. Lord, have mercy
c. Body of Christ
d. get that in your spirit
e. go with God

5. He was Caesar when Christ was born:
    a. Augustus
    b. Julius
    c. Claudius
    d. Vespasian
    e. Nero

6. He was Caesar when Christ was crucified:
    a. Augustus
    b. Maximus Thrax
    c. Constantine
    d. Diocletian
    e. Tiberius

7. What does the Latin word *credo*, from which the English word "creed" is derived, mean?
    a. One God
    b. Faith
    c. I believe
    d. Belief
    e. Credibility

8. Once widely called "devil's brew," this beverage was eventually approved by Pope Clement VIII in 1595:
    a. rum
    b. vodka
    c. whiskey

d. coffee
e. wine coolers

9. The *Catechism* describes actual grace as:
    a. a stable disposition of the will
    b. God's interventions
    c. a supernatural disposition
    d. a permanent indwelling of grace
    e. prayer before actual meals

10. Who was the first pope to fly in an airplane?
    a. Pius XII
    b. John XXIII
    c. Paul VI
    d. John Paul I
    e. John Paul II

11. Who devised the basis of the dividing epochs of time into B.C. and A.D.?
    a. St. Irenaeus of Lyons
    b. James Ussher, Protestant bishop of Armagh, Ireland
    c. Pope St. Damasus I
    d. Dionysius Exiguus
    e. Albertus Magnus

12. What does the slang term getting a "Golden Sombrero" refer to?
    a. when a bishop is promoted to archbishop
    b. when an archbishop is promoted to cardinal
    c. when a baseball player strikes out four times in one game
    d. when a bishop is invited to throw the first pitch of a new baseball season
    e. when a person who has been beatified moves up a notch upon being canonized a saint

A POTPOURRI OF POPERY

Answer Key

1. B. Ha ha! Saint Philip Neri was never pope, but he probably would have laughed at the very thought of it. And yes, seriously, there really was a Pope Hilarius (died 468), though history does not reveal whether he lived up to his name or not. But we do know Pope John XXIII liked a good laugh. Some examples: "In reply to a reporter who asked, 'How many people work in the Vatican?', he reportedly said: 'About half of them.' Also, "When a cardinal complained that an [increase] in Vatican salaries meant a particular usher earned as much as the cardinal, the pope remarked: 'That usher has 10 children; I hope the cardinal doesn't!'" ("Pope John XXIII Lived with a Keen Sense of Humor," *Catholic Herald*, catholicherald.org).

2. D. "Pater noster" is the Latin translation of the first words of "The Our Father" prayer taught by Jesus to His disciples in Matthew 6:9-13 and Luke 11:2-4, which makes it the oldest Christian prayer. While the first words of the *Hail Mary* uttered by the Angel Gabriel (Luke 1:28) are older, they came *before* the Incarnation of Christ and were not originally a prayer, but the Angel's formal greeting to Our Lady.

3. C. Pope from 1846-1878, he holds the record as the second longest pontificate in history at 31 years, seven months, and 23 days (Saint Peter, the first pope, is first at circa 35 years). Among other accomplishments, Pius IX defined the dogma of Mary's Immaculate Conception (her perpetual preservation from sin) in 1854, and convened the First Vatican Council in 1868, which resulted in the definition of the dogma of papal infallibility. See John Burger, "The First Pope to Be Photographed Was Not Afraid of New Technology," at aleteia.com.

4. B. The very first Mass was the Last Supper, and the Lord spoke to His Apostles there in either Hebrew or Aramaic or a combination

of both. Soon after the Ascension, as the Church began in earnest her predominant *lingua franca* of the East (a common language or "bridge language"), the ancient Mass quickly took root in that language, while in the West Latin predominated. The *Kyrie Eleison* prayer is a precious reminder of the Greek roots of the Mass. The Catholic Church also preserves in the Mass Hebrew words such as *hôsî-âh-nā* (transliterated into Greek as *hosanna*), *Amen*, and *hallelujah*.

5. A. The grand-nephew of Julius Caesar, his reign and rise to power was fraught with civil wars and ruthless, violent retribution toward enemies, and other dirty deeds done dirt cheap. Many of the events of his reign are recorded in Christian history, the most notable being his call for a census, which resulted in Jesus' birth in Bethlehem (Lk. 2:1).

6. E. The martyrdom of John the Baptist also occurred within Tiberius' reign (Lk. 3:1).

7. C. Both the Nicene Creed and the shorter Apostles Creed begin with the word *credo* in Latin. Publicly professing your Catholic Faith via creed is a venerable custom with roots in the earliest Church.

8. D. Coffee, which has "been a source of contention for rulers, clerics, and citizens," gained popularity among Muslims within the Ottoman Empire in the fifteenth century. The first coffee shop opened in 1457 to meet the demand for its taste and assistance in focusing for long hours of study or prayer. The story says that Pope Clement VIII gave it a try when banning "the devil's brew" was brought to his attention; he decided that it was "so delicious that it would be a pity to let the infidels have exclusive use of it" and proceeded to "bless" coffee so it could be enjoyed by the Church as well ("Suave Molecules of Mocha: Coffee, Chemistry, and Civilization." Hannah Meyers, 2005).

9. B. The *Catechism* tells us of three kinds of graces: sanctifying grace, habitual grace and actual grace. Sanctifying grace is "an habitual gift" that adheres to the soul to enable it to be receptive to God. Habitual grace is a "permanent disposition" that inclines us to pursue God's call for us. Actual grace, then, is direct intervention by God, often seen in sudden conversions or seemingly random "lightbulb" experiences in your faith journey (*Catechism of the Catholic Church*, 2000).

10. C. In 1965, he "was the first [pope] to travel by airplane, the first to leave Italy since 1809, and the first to visit all continents." See Daniel Esparza, "The First Pope Who Traveled by Plane" at aleteia.com.

11. D. He died circa 544. "[L]earned in both Greek and Latin, and an accomplished Scripturist. Much of his life was spent in Rome, where he governed a monastery as abbot.... Dionysius has left his mark conspicuously, for it was he who introduced the use of the Christian Era [A.D.] according to which dates are reckoned from the Incarnation [of Christ] . . . By this method of computation he intended to supersede the 'Era of [the pagan Roman Emperor] Diocletian' previously employed, being unwilling, as he tells us, that the name of an impious persecutor should be thus kept in memory" ("Dionysius Exiguus," *Catholic Encyclopedia*, vol. V, p. 10-11).

12. C. Notable MLB players inducted into this dubious group include Reggie Jackson, Sammy Sosa, and Bo Jackson.

Man and Wife, Say Man and Wife

How much do YOU know about Big Fat Catholic Weddings?

1. Who told her daughter to ask for the head of John the Baptist?
    a. Naomi
    b. Herodias
    c. Jezebel
    d. Deborah
    e. Sapphira

2. Which of the following conditions is *not* necessary for some sacraments?
    a. an outward sign
    b. instituted by Christ
    c. administered by a priest or deacon
    d. conferred in a Catholic church or chapel
    e. C & D

3. Which married couple helped St. Paul establish the Catholic church in Corinth?
    a. Aquila and Priscilla
    b. Silas and Lydia
    c. Ananias and Sapphira
    d. St. Peter and his (unnamed) wife
    e. Cornelius and Tabitha

4. Who is considered the patron saint of those who want to be married?
    a. St. Anne

b. St. Joseph
c. St. Mary Magdalene
d. St. Raphael
e. that woman who sang, "Why Won't You Marry Me, Bill?" in the 1969 hit song *Wedding Bell Blues*

5. What does the word *catholic* mean, as it appears in the Nicene Creed?
    a. for the whole
    b. called forth
    c. Body of Christ
    d. assembly
    e. ruled by bishops

6. What is the valid "form and matter" of the sacrament of holy matrimony?
    a. The man and woman exchanging mutual consent to marriage and their pronouncing of the wedding vows
    b. The exchange of the rings and the blessing of the priest (or deacon)
    c. The pronouncing of the wedding vows and the bride's and groom's first official kiss
    d. The priest's blessing of the couple and their lighting of the unity candle
    e. The opening lines of the ceremony are, "Mawwiage. Mawwiage is what bwings us togevah today..."

7. Which of the following is *not* an impediment (obstacle) to a valid celebration of the sacrament of Holy Matrimony?
    a. Neither the bride nor the groom has any intention of ever having any children (*inconceivable!*)
    b. The groom intentionally conceals from the bride that he is seriously addicted to meth

c. The bride intentionally conceals from the groom the fact that she had been sterilized
d. The bride despises a member of the groom's family and refuses to let that person attend the wedding
e. The bride and groom are closely related by law or blood (consanguinity)

8. All right then, who is the Patron Saint of *engaged* couples?
    a. St. Agnes
    b. St. Mary Magdalene
    c. St. Valentine
    d. a and c
    e. none of the above

9. The word *ekklesía*, which we translate into English as "church," derives from:
    a. Latin
    b. Greek
    c. Aramaic
    d. Hebrew
    e. Old Spanish

10. According to the Bible, approximately how many wives did King Solomon have?
    a. 57
    b. 144
    c. 486
    d. 700
    e. only one wife; King Solomon was a wise man.

11. A deacon is:
    a. A priest who does not have permission to celebrate Mass until after his wife dies

b. A layman who may distribute Communion, marry people, baptize babies, and wear vestments when called upon to do so by a bishop
c. A man who has received the first level of holy orders and is neither a priest nor a layman
d. Forbidden to hear confessions and give absolution except in emergency situations and in the absence of a priest
e. None of the above

12. Which of the following nuts is/are mentioned by name in the Bible?
    a. almonds
    b. cashews
    c. peanuts
    d. pecans
    e. walnuts

Answer Key

1. B. This sordid story is recounted in Matthew 14:1-12, Mark 6:14-29, and Luke 3:18-20. His refusal to compromise and "go along to get along" is a reminder for those facing the painful dilemma of being invited to attend the wedding of a Catholic family member or friend entering into an invalid "marriage."

2. E. A layperson can validly baptize using the valid form and matter and having the intention to baptize as the Church does. The husband and wife confer the sacrament of Holy Matrimony upon each other. Although it is customary to celebrate the sacraments inside a Catholic church or chapel, it is not an absolute requirement (except for the canonical form of a marriage, but that requirement too has exceptions). Indeed, all the sacraments can be validly and licitly conferred anywhere (think of celebrating Mass

on battlefields or Catholic priests hearing the confessions of and granting absolution to fellow passengers on the sinking Titanic).

3. A. See Acts 18:18-26, Romans 16:3, 1 Corinthians 16:19.

4. B. Pope Saint John Paul II wrote his apostolic exhortation *Guardian of the Redeemer* (*Redemptoris Custos*) as a paean to Saint Joseph as a model of a most chaste spouse to Our Lady and a noble and courageous foster father to Jesus. Thus he is the perfect patron saint for all men and women seeking a happy and holy marriage: "At the culmination of the history of salvation, when God reveals his love for humanity through the gift of the Word, it is precisely the marriage of Mary and Joseph that brings to realization in full 'freedom' the 'spousal gift of self' in receiving and expressing such a love" (7).

5. A. "Catholic" means universal. It comes from the Greek compound word καθολικός (*katholokós*), derived from καθό (*kathó* = "according to") and ὅλος (*holos* = "the whole"). Although we don't know when, where, or by whom the term "catholic" was first used as the formal name for the Church Jesus established, we know that it had become common usage among Christians by the beginning of the second century. The word "catholic" conveyed the Church's mission is for all people, in all places, at all times. Around the year A.D. 345, Saint Cyril of Jerusalem commented on the meaning and importance of the name "catholic": "And if ever thou art sojourning in any city, inquire not simply where the "Lord's house"' is...nor merely where the "church"' is, but where is the *Catholic Church*. For this is the peculiar name of the holy body, the mother of us all.... Now [the Church] is called Catholic because it is throughout the world, from one end of the earth to the other'" (*Catechetical Lectures* 26, 23; *Answer Me This*, 29).

6. A. See Nicholas Halligan, O.P., *The Sacraments and Their Celebration*, pp. 58-59 (Wipf & Stock, 1986).

7. D. See: *The Sacraments and Their Celebration*, pp. 171-190 (Wipf & Stock, 1986).

8. D. Agnes (circa A.D. 304) is venerated as a virgin and martyr who accepted martyrdom *in defense of* her virginity as a teenager. *Butler's Lives of the Saints* says that "her riches and beauty excited the young noblemen of the first families of Rome to contend as rivals for her hand [in marriage]. Agnes answered them all that she had consecrated her virginity to her heavenly husband [Jesus], who could not be beheld by mortal eyes. Her suitors, finding her resolution unshakable, accused her to the governor as a Christian" (Christian Classics, Allen, TX, 1996; vol. I, p. 133). She refused the governor's command to marry, even on threat of torture. After a man was struck blind for trying to harm her (and was healed when she prayed for him), the governor decided she was to be beheaded forthwith. St. Ambrose writes, "She went to the place of execution more cheerfully than others go to their wedding" (*Catholic Encyclopedia*, vol. I, p. 214).

9. B. It means an "assembly" or a "congregation" and appears several times in the Septuagint Greek translation of the Hebrew Old Testament. When Jesus said, "Upon this rock I will build my Church," *ekklesía* took on a distinctive meaning for Christians as *the* unique assembly of believers. It appears in its various forms over 200 times in the New Testament.

10. D. And he had an additional 300 concubines! See 1 Kings 11:3.

11. C. *Catechism of the Catholic Church,* 1570: "Deacons share in Christ's mission and grace in a special way. The sacrament of Holy Orders marks them with an imprint ('character') which cannot be removed and which configures them to Christ, who made himself the 'deacon' or servant of all. Among other tasks, it is the task of deacons to assist the bishop and priests in the celebration of the divine mysteries, above all the Eucharist, in the distribution

of Holy Communion, in assisting at and blessing marriages, in the proclamation of the Gospel and preaching, in presiding over funerals, and in dedicating themselves to the various ministries of charity."

12. A. Genesis 43:11.

Founders Keepers

There's something for everyone in the Catholic Faith, and these pioneering Catholics made sure of that by establishing new religious orders, groups, and pious devotions.

1. Who founded the University of Notre Dame?
    a. Knute Rockne
    b. Fr. Edward Flanagan
    c. Fr. Edward Sorin
    d. Fr. Edward McGillicuddy
    e. Our Lady herself, when she swung by Indiana on one of her many trips

2. Who founded the Knights of Columbus?
    a. Blessed Fr. Michael J. McGivney
    b. Msgr. Francis X. Duffy
    c. Bishop John Ireland
    d. Venerable Archbishop Fulton J. Sheen
    e. Cardinal Francis Spellman

3. What early heresy affirmed the divinity of Christ but denied his true humanity?
    a. Gnostic Docetism
    b. Arianism
    c. Monophysitism
    d. Nestorianism
    e. Arianism

4. Who founded the Catholic Missions in China?
   a. Francis Xavier
   b. Matteo Ricci
   c. Junipero Serra (in his spare time)
   d. Nicolás Bobadilla
   e. George R. Binks (say it 3 times fast)

5. What word or phrase in the Creed is a point of contention even today between the Catholic and Orthodox Churches?
   a. *protoevangelium*
   b. *credo in unum Deo*
   c. *Theotókos*
   d. *filioque*
   e. Carne asada tacos are the best tacos in the world

6. When did the East-West Schism in the Church occur, resulting in what is known as the Eastern Orthodox Churches that are separated from the Catholic Church?
   a. 989
   b. 1054
   c. 1066
   d. 1517
   e. 1492

7. Which Catholic Spaniard is credited as being one of the founding fathers of the State of California?
   a. Junipero Serra
   b. Hernán Cortés
   c. Vasco Nuñez de Balboa
   d. Juan Rodríguez Cabrillo
   e. Juan Ponce de León

8. The heresy of Arianism denied the divinity of Christ. But, which of the following denied the divinity of the Holy Spirit?
    a. Nestorianism
    b. Pneumatokarentism
    c. Pelagianism
    d. Pneumatomachians
    e. Monothelitism

9. What error did the heresy of Utraquism entail?
    a. The denial of the uniqueness of Jesus Christ as messiah and redeemer
    b. The denial that Latin (a dead language) is a suitable official language for papal encyclicals
    c. The claim that one must receive the Holy Eucharist under both kinds in order to receive "all of Jesus"
    d. The assertion that the Second Coming won't happen until Relevant Radio has at least one radio station in each country of the world
    e. The belief that Catholics can ignore the Church's canonical form and get married validly in a ceremony at the beach, or a country club, or taco shop.

10. This is the founder of the St. Vincent de Paul Society:
    a. St. Vincent de Paul
    b. Pauline Jericot
    c. Bl. Frédéric Ozanam
    d. St. Mother Cabrini
    e. St. Vincent Ferrer

11. This heresy entails opposition to or even the destruction of sacred images:
    a. docetism
    b. gnosticism

c. smashionalism
   d. Rosicrucianism
   e. iconoclasm

12. Who was the founder of the religious order known as the Salesians?
    a. St. John Bosco
    b. Fr. Edward Flanagan
    c. St. Francis de Sales
    d. St. Joseph of Cupertino
    e. Frank Sheed

Answer Key

1. C. 1814-1893, and he wasn't even Irish! (He was born in the small French town of Ahuillé, almost 200 miles from Paris).

2. A. 1852-1890, born in Waterbury, Connecticut. Ordained a priest in Baltimore in 1877 and created the Knights of Columbus with three principles in mind: active charity, faithful unity, and fraternal connection. He was declared venerable by Pope Benedict XVI for his immense contribution to the growth of Catholicism in the United States in 2008 and beatified in 2020.

3. C. This heresy was condemned at the First Council of Ephesus in A.D. 431 by affirming that Christ is a divine person (i.e., the second Person of the Blessed Trinity) with a divine nature *and*, in the Incarnation, a perfect human nature.

4. B. "Born at Macerata in the Papal States, October 6, 1552; died at Peking, May 11, 1610.... Matteo Ricci remains a splendid type of missionary and founder, unsurpassed for his zealous intrepidity, the intelligence of the methods applied to each situation, and the unwearying tenacity with which he pursued the projects he

undertook. To him belongs the glory not only of opening up a vast empire [of China] to the Gospel, but of simultaneously making the first breach in that distrust of strangers which excluded China from the general progress of the world" ("Matteo Ricci," *Catholic Encyclopedia*, vol. XIII, pp. 34-39).

5. D. The Latin word *"filioque" (fee-lee-OH-kwe)* is translated into English as "and the son," in that, as the Catholic creed says, the Holy Spirit proceeds "from the Father and the son." This one word, added by Western Catholics to the Creed (which does not originally have "and the son" in the original Greek or in the Latin) has been the source of Orthodox opposition for over the last thousand years. It's a complex and important issue that's beyond the space available in this book to adequately discuss, but I explain it further in my book *Answer Me This!* (Our Sunday Visitor, 2003), pp. 122-127. Ludwig Ott says, "That the Holy Ghost proceeds from the Father and from the Son as from One Single Principle and through One Single spiration [i.e., breathing out], is clear from John 16:15: 'All that the Father has is mine.' If the Son, by virtue of his eternal generation from the Father, possesses everything that the Father possesses, except the Fatherhood and the unregeneratedness, which are not communicable, then He must also possess the power of spiration, and with it the being a principle in relation to the Holy Ghost" (Ibid., p. 124-125).

6. B. For a non-polemical historical overview of this disastrous schism, see Aidan Nichols, O.P., *Rome and the Eastern Churches: A Study in Schism* (The Liturgical Press, Collegeville, MN, 1992). For an admittedly more apologetics-oriented approach, try *Ending the Byzantine Greek Schism*, written by James Likoudis, a convert to the Catholic Church from Eastern Orthodoxy.

7. A. 1713-1784, St. Junipero Serra was born in Majorca, Spain and served for years as a professor of philosophy there and in Mexico

before embarking on his life's work of evangelizing the indigenous peoples of California and establishing for them a series of commercial and agricultural outposts (with military protection) that became known as the California Missions, now numbering 21. When I was attending grammar school at Mission San Juan Capistrano, I was privileged to serve as an altar boy in the traditional daily Latin Mass in the Old Mission's "Serra Chapel," the only still extant chapel in which Serra himself celebrated Mass.

8. D. "A heretical sect which flourished in the countries adjacent to the Hellespont (i.e., the Dardanelles) during the latter half of the fourth, and the beginning of the fifth century. They denied the divinity of the Holy Ghost, hence the name Pneumatomachi or Combators against the Spirit" ("Pneumatomachi," *Catholic Encyclopedia*, vol. 12, p. 174).

9. C. Derived at least indirectly from the errors of John Wyclif (1324-1384), "Utraquism . . . means this: Man, in order to be saved, must receive Holy Communion when he wishes and where he wishes, under the forms of bread *and* wine (*sub utraque specie*)" ("Utraquism," *Catholic Encyclopedia*, vol. XV, p. 144. Emphasis added.).

10. C. I'll bet you guessed "St. Vincent de Paul," didn't you? Turns out, it was actually Blessed Antoine-Frédéric Ozanam, "born at Milan, April 23, 1813; died at Marseilles, September 8, 1853.... A brilliant apologist, impressed by the benefits of the Christian religion, he desired that they should be made known to all who might read his works or hear his words." The Society of St. Vincent de Paul was established as "an international association of Catholic laymen engaging systematically in personal service of the poor; was founded in May, 1833,... whose object should be to minister to the wants of the Parisian poor. The master-mind conceiving the project, which was destined to make an indelible im-

press upon the history of modern charity work, was Frédéric Ozanam, a brilliant young Frenchman, lawyer, author and professor in the Sorbonne" ("Society of Saint Vincent de Paul," *Catholic Encyclopedia*, vol. XI, p. 378; vol. XIII, p. 389).

11. E. "'Iconoclasm' (from the Greek word meaning 'image-breaking') is a heresy that opposes the use of religious images, which are called 'icons' in the Eastern Church. Iconoclasm manifests itself in virtually all Protestant denominations as well as in religions as diverse as Islam, Mormonism, and the Jehovah's Witnesses. Modern-day iconoclasts condemn the Catholic custom of venerating religious statues, pictures, and crucifixes as 'idolatry.' . . . Iconoclasts appeal to a variety of Bible verses and argue that God has forbidden the fashioning of images for religious purposes. Exodus 20:3–6 . . . 'You shall not have other gods besides me. You shall not carve idols for yourselves in the shape of anything in the sky above or on the earth below or in the waters beneath the earth; you shall not bow down before them.' [Also], Deuteronomy 5:8, Isaiah 44:9–20 and 45:20, Jeremiah 7:30, John 4:24, and Romans 1:23–24. Such verses, when read in context, . . . reiterate the constant Catholic position that idol-worship is gravely sinful. [But there are] many other biblical verses in which God permits and even *commands* the carving of statues and other images for religious purposes. Consider Exodus 25:18–22, 28:33–34, and 37:7–9; Numbers 21:8–9; 1 Kings 6:23–28 and 7:23–29; and 2 Chronicles chapters 3 — 5" (Patrick Madrid, *Envoy for Christ: 25 Years as a Catholic Apologist*, 2012, Servant Books, pp. 72-74, emphasis added).

12. A. (1815-1888) As a young priest, one of St. John Bosco's (a.k.a. Don Bosco) "duties was to accompany Don Cafasso upon his visits to the prisons of the city, and the condition of the children confined in these places, abandoned to the most evil influences, and with little before them but the gallows, made such an indeli-

ble impression upon his mind that he resolved to devote his life to the rescue of these unfortunate outcasts.... [in 1852] he was urged to consolidate and perpetuate his work by forming a religious congregation, and in 1857 he drew up its first set of rules. In the following year he went to Rome to seek the advice and support of his benefactor, Pope Pius IX, and in 1859 he summoned the first chapter of the congregation, and began the Society of Saint Francis de Sales (the Salesians)" (*Catholic Encyclopedia*, "Salesian Society" and "St. Giovanni Melchior Bosco," vol. II, p. 689, vol. XIII, pp. 398-399).

In a World of Churches, Be a Cathedral

Even if some of its members are sinful and sometimes obnoxious, the Catholic Church Herself, as founded by Jesus Christ, is beautiful, inside and out. Her doctrines and venerable legacy of building beautiful churches in which to worship God have a long and beautiful history.

1. What does the term "tetragrammaton" mean?
    a. the four cardinal virtues
    b. It's the biblical Greek word for "great grandmother"
    c. the first four books of the Old Testament canon
    d. the 4 Hebrew consonants which substitute the name of God in Scripture
    e. a package of 12 shapes that you can fit together, like Tetris blocks

2. This saint, who was known to levitate while in ecstasies of prayer, is considered the patron of astronauts:
    a. St. Albert the Great
    b. St. Bernard of Clairvaux
    c. St. Maria Goretti
    d. St. Dunstan the Lofty
    e. St. Joseph of Cupertino

3. What's the difference between a cathedral and a basilica?
    a. cathedrals are bigger
    b. while some churches are designated basilicas, cathedrals are automatically basilicas

c. there's no difference; Catholics call their big churches "cathedrals" and the Greek Orthodox call theirs "basilicas"
d. traditionally, the top two or three parish churches that produce the most priestly vocations in a diocese get the honor of being named basilicas
e. any Catholic church could, in theory, be designated a basilica, but a cathedral is the official church of a diocesan bishop

4. Who was the first bishop of the United States?
    a. John Neumann
    b. Lewis Carroll
    c. Charles Carroll
    d. John Carroll
    e. Carroll O'Connor

5. Where was the first diocese established in the United States?
    a. Boston
    b. Baltimore
    c. New York
    d. Washington
    e. St. Augustine

6. Which of the following founders of a major religious order was never ordained to the priesthood?
    a. St. Benedict
    b. St. Dominic
    c. St. Ignatius of Loyola
    d. St. Alphonsus Liguori
    e. St. Francis of Assisi

In a World of Churches, Be a Cathedral

Even if some of its members are sinful and sometimes obnoxious, the Catholic Church Herself, as founded by Jesus Christ, is beautiful, inside and out. Her doctrines and venerable legacy of building beautiful churches in which to worship God have a long and beautiful history.

1. What does the term "tetragrammaton" mean?
    a. the four cardinal virtues
    b. It's the biblical Greek word for "great grandmother"
    c. the first four books of the Old Testament canon
    d. the 4 Hebrew consonants which substitute the name of God in Scripture
    e. a package of 12 shapes that you can fit together, like Tetris blocks

2. This saint, who was known to levitate while in ecstasies of prayer, is considered the patron of astronauts:
    a. St. Albert the Great
    b. St. Bernard of Clairvaux
    c. St. Maria Goretti
    d. St. Dunstan the Lofty
    e. St. Joseph of Cupertino

3. What's the difference between a cathedral and a basilica?
    a. cathedrals are bigger
    b. while some churches are designated basilicas, cathedrals are automatically basilicas

c. there's no difference; Catholics call their big churches "cathedrals" and the Greek Orthodox call theirs "basilicas"
   d. traditionally, the top two or three parish churches that produce the most priestly vocations in a diocese get the honor of being named basilicas
   e. any Catholic church could, in theory, be designated a basilica, but a cathedral is the official church of a diocesan bishop

4. Who was the first bishop of the United States?
   a. John Neumann
   b. Lewis Carroll
   c. Charles Carroll
   d. John Carroll
   e. Carroll O'Connor

5. Where was the first diocese established in the United States?
   a. Boston
   b. Baltimore
   c. New York
   d. Washington
   e. St. Augustine

6. Which of the following founders of a major religious order was never ordained to the priesthood?
   a. St. Benedict
   b. St. Dominic
   c. St. Ignatius of Loyola
   d. St. Alphonsus Liguori
   e. St. Francis of Assisi

7. The English word *monk* comes from a Greek word that means:
    a. alone
    b. bald
    c. celibate
    d. silence
    e. funny haircut

8. Which pope promulgated the landmark encyclical *Humanae Vitae*?
    a. Pius XI
    b. Pius XII
    c. St. John XXIII
    d. St. Paul VI
    e. John Paul I

9. Which pope extended the Feast of the Sacred Heart to be observed by the Universal Church?
    a. Pius VIII
    b. Pius IX
    c. Pius X
    d. Pius XI
    e. Leo XIII

10. Wisdom, understanding, counsel, strength, knowledge, joy, and fear of the Lord are traditionally known as what?
    a. the gifts of the Holy Spirit
    b. the fruits of the Holy Spirit
    c. the cardinal virtues
    d. virtual virtues
    e. the fruits of listening to Relevant Radio every day

11. Which supernatural virtue specifically protects you from discouragement and despair?
    a. faith
    b. hope
    c. perseverance
    d. charity
    e. fortitude

12. The Church teaches that the most painful punishment of the damned is:
    a. hellish heat
    b. numbing cold
    c. frightening demons
    d. the pain of eternal loss of God
    e. no wi-fi

Answer Key

1. D. Derived from the Hebrew consonants (YHWH) of the name God gave to Moses in Exodus 3:13:15, "I AM WHO AM." The *Encyclopedia Judaica* notes that "[e]very time [the high priest] uttered the holy name of God, the Tetragrammaton, which was uttered only on the Day of Atonement, the people prostrated themselves and responded: "Blessed be His Name whose glorious kingdom is forever and ever" (vol. 2, p. 744).

2. E. St. Joseph of Cupertino was portrayed by Maximilian Schell in the 1962 movie *The Reluctant Saint*.

3. E. The English word "cathedral" derives from the Greek καθέδρα (*kathédra*), which means "chair." This same word appears in the Greek in Matthew 23:2, where Jesus says, "The scribes and the Pharisees sit on Moses' *seat* [*kathédra*]; so practice and observe

whatever they tell you, but not what they do..." The "seat of Moses" was a literal stone chair in which the rabbis would sit as a symbol of their teaching authority. Jesus invokes the binding authority of a Jewish *oral tradition* here not found in the Old Testament Scriptures. The Church adopted this symbolism by having a literal *kathédra* in churches where a bishop resided, and thus, these churches became known as *cathedrals* because they were where a bishop's seat was located. The word "see" (as in the "Holy See," or as a synonym for "diocese") is also a synonym for "chair." And finally, the Latin phrase "*ex cathedra*" in reference to an extraordinary exercise of papal infallibility means . . . well, by now you should be able to finish that sentence by yourself!

4. D. 1735-1815, Carroll was born in Maryland about 15 miles east of what is now Washington, DC. In an unusual move, Pope Pius VI invited the priests in that area to choose the site of the first cathedral (Baltimore) and nominate one of their own to be their first bishop. He approved their choice of John Carroll in 1798 ("John Carroll," *Catholic Encyclopedia* (1908), vol. 3, p. 382).

5. B. "Established as a diocese 6 April, 1789; as an archdiocese 8 April, 1808" ("Archdiocese of Baltimore," *Catholic Encyclopedia*, vol II, p. 228).

6. E. 1181-1226, born in Assisi (where else?!). Although Francis founded one of the largest and most important Catholic religious orders of men and women in the history of the Church, out of humility, he never sought to be ordained a priest, but was ordained to the diaconate later in life.

7. A. The Greek word μόνος (*mónos*) means "alone" or "solitary." Thus, the noun μοναχός (*monachós*) denotes "one who is alone," a term applied to hermits and monks from antiquity. In A.D. 360, St. Athanasius (circa 296-393) wrote a magnificent biography of the greatest of all monks, Saint Anthony the Great (251-356),

renowned for a long life (he lived to be 105!) of asceticism, prayer, and profound spiritual insights gained while fasting, praying, and engaging in dramatic spiritual combat in a cave in the Egyptian desert.

8. D. After several years of consulting medical and theological experts on the topic of contraception, the pope issued *Humanae Vitae* 1968 as a clear and much needed reaffirmation of the Catholic Church's continuous teaching that contraception, abortifacient drugs, sterilization (e.g., vasectomies and tubal ligations), and "any action which either before, at the moment of, or after . . . is specifically intended to prevent procreation—whether as an end or as a means," is intrinsically evil and thus a mortal sin. (See *Humanae Vitae* 14).

9. B. He did this in 1856. Pope Leo XIII continued to up the ante on the devotion, writing an Act of Consecration to the Sacred Heart in 1899 and approving the Scapular of the Sacred Heart at the turn of the century.

10. A. See CCC 1285–1287, 1830–1831, and 1845. In Scripture: Isaiah 11:2-3 and 1 Corinthians 12:7-11 ("manifestations of the Spirit").

11. B. CCC 1818: "The virtue of hope responds to the aspiration to happiness which God has placed in the heart of every man... it keeps man from discouragement; it sustains him during times of abandonment; it opens up his heart in expectation of eternal beatitude. Buoyed up by hope, he is preserved from selfishness and led to the happiness that flows from charity."

12. D. The *Catholic Encyclopedia* says, "The *poena damni*, or pain of loss, consists in the loss of the beatific vision and in so complete a separation of all the powers of the soul from God that it cannot find in Him even the least peace and rest....The desire for happiness inherent in their very nature, wholly unsatisfied and no

longer able to find any compensation for the loss of God in delusive pleasure, renders them utterly miserable. The pain of loss is the very core of eternal punishment" ("Hell," vol. VII, p. 210).

Holy Dynamic Duos!

Saints and Doctors of the Church come in all shapes and sizes – and sometimes, they even come in pairs. Brother and sister, husband and wife, parent and child, devoted friends like Saints Francis and Clare... and, in the case of St. Jerome and Eusebius, cave buddies (literal "man caves" in the early Church!). How many of these holy pairs and patrons can you name?

1. She was St. John of the Cross' dear friend and collaborator:
    a. St. Thérèse of the Child Jesus
    b. St. Teresa of Avila
    c. St. Teresa of the Andes
    d. St. Teresa Benedicta of the Cross
    e. St. Teresa of Calcutta

2. Who was a dear friend and fellow Saint of St. Francis de Sales?
    a. Teresa of Avila
    b. Catherine of Siena
    c. Jane Frances de Chantal
    d. Juliana Falconieri
    e. La Shanta Boufanté

3. Who translated the Bible from Hebrew and Greek into Latin, giving us what is known as the Vulgate?
    a. St. Augustine
    b. St. John Chrysostom
    c. Origen
    d. St. Jerome
    e. Pope St. Damasus I

4. Who was the wife of St. Isidore the Farmer (a.k.a. Isidore the Worker) and is herself venerated unofficially as a Saint?
    a. Maria Torribia
    b. Maria the Farmer
    c. Su Merced Doña Nancy Weinberger de Madrid
    d. Isidora Obreragranja
    e. Marisol Carmen Pilar Dolores Consuelo Magdalena Rosa Alejandra Isabela Judita Zuñiga y Todolodemasco-moese (whew)

5. Who was the saintly sister of St. Benedict?
    a. Gertrude
    b. Ursula
    c. Benedicta
    d. Scholastica
    e. Monastica

6. Canonized in 1992, this Jesuit saint was the spiritual director to St. Margaret Mary Alacoque:
    a. Isaac Jogues
    b. Aloysius Gonzaga
    c. John Berchmans
    d. Claude la Colombière
    e. Peter Canisius

7. Had this Frankish Catholic military ruler not been victorious at the Battle of Tours, the Muslims probably would have conquered Western Europe:
    a. Don Juan of Austria
    b. Charlemagne
    c. St. John Capistrano
    d. Charles Martel
    e. St. Martin of Tours

8. He is the patron saint of altar boys:
    a. St. Aloysius Gonzaga
    b. St. John Berchmans
    c. St. Charles Borromeo
    d. St. Dominic Savio
    e. St. Pancratius

9. Aside from St. Patrick, who are other official patron saints of Ireland?
    a. St. Killian and St. Guinness
    b. St. Bede the Venerable and St. George
    c. St. Columba and St. Brigid of Kildare
    d. St. Oliver Plunkett
    e. St. Patrick is *the* official patron saint

10. Which of the following British authors was *never* Anglican?
    a. G.K. Chesterton
    b. E. E. Evans-Pritchard
    c. T.S. Eliot
    d. C.S. Lewis
    e. J.R.R. Tolkien

11. Which medieval Benedictine monk is regarded as the inventor of modern musical notation?
    a. St. Gregory the Great
    b. Guido d'Arezzo
    c. Peter Abelard
    d. St. Meinrad
    e. St. Bernard of Clairvaux

12. He was selected pope because a dove landed on him and it was taken as a sign from God:

HOLY DYNAMIC DUOS!

    a. Fabian
    b. Sebastian
    c. Theodore
    d. Victor
    e. Sergius

Answer Key

1. B. (1515-1582) St. Teresa of Avila was born in ... (wait for it) ... Avila, Spain. Her religious name was Teresa of Jesus, she was a towering figure of Catholic mystical theology. After she had entered religious life, she was given by God in a vision the awareness of her own lukewarmness and experienced a profound conversion, after which she not only lived out her life as a religious sister with deep fervor, but she undertook a massive reform of the Carmelite order amidst many trials and much opposition. She wrote a powerful little meditation I like to quote: "Let nothing disturb you. Let nothing frighten you. All things are passing away. God never changes. Patience obtains all things. Whoever has God lacks nothing. God alone suffices." Get *that* in your spirit!

2. C. (1572-1641) St. Jane Frances de Chantal was born in Dijon, France, into a wealthy, noble family. Married at 20 and widowed at 28, she chose not to remarry but to raise her children while at the same time pursuing a life of good deeds, almsgiving, and service to the poor. She befriended St. Francis de Sales, then bishop of Geneva, and became his spiritual directee, eventually entering the convent and later establishing her own religious order, the Sisters of the Visitation. She was canonized in 1776.

3. D. (340-420) Jerome was born in the Roman town of Stridon (in modern-day Croatia or Bosnia-Herzegovina). Renowned as a

master of Latin, Greek, and Hebrew, he was deeply knowledgeable of Holy Scripture. The towering importance of his new translation of the Old and New Testaments into Latin cannot be underestimated. Pope Damasus commissioned Jerome to update the New Testament in Latin, and the saint did, comparing it alongside unique and ancient Greek manuscripts to ensure its accuracy. "[We have] no manuscript copies... older than St. Jerome's Latin translation made on then ancient copies." (*Catholic Encyclopedia*, "Vulgate," vol. XV, pp. 515-516). In 386 St. Jerome retired to a cave in Bethlehem and spent the remainder of his long life there working on other biblical translations, works of exegesis and apologetics, and a voluminous correspondence.

4. A. (Died 1175) Although not yet canonized (maybe someday?), she is known more popularly in Spain as Santa María de la Cabeza.

5. D. Some believe Scholastica and Benedict were twins, but what we know for certain is that they were very close. The last time they met was three days before Scholastica's death, and she begged Benedict to stay with her. Not wanting to keep his fellow monks out of the monastery overnight, he refused. Pope St. Gregory the Great details what happened next: "bowing her head upon [her folded hands], she made her prayers to Almighty God, and lifting her head from the table, there fell suddenly such a tempest of [lightning] and thundering, and such abundance of rain, that neither venerable Benedict, nor the monks that were with him, could put their head out of door. Three days later, Benedict beheld the soul of his sister, which was departed from her body, in the likeness of a dove, to ascend into heaven: who rejoicing much to see her great glory, with hymns and lauds gave thanks to Almighty God, and did impart news of this her death to his monks whom also he sent presently to bring her corpse to his abbey, to have it buried in that grave which he had provided for himself" (*Dia-*

logues, vol. II).

6. D. Jesuit priest, born in France in 1641, died 1682. He was canonized in 1992 by Pope St. John Paul II.

7. D. (688-741) "In October, 732, Charles met Abd-er-Rahman outside of Tours and defeated and slew him in the Battle of Poitiers, which must ever remain one of the great events in the history of the world, as upon its issue depended whether Christian Civilization should continue or Islam prevail throughout Europe. It was this battle, it is said, that gave Charles his name, Martel 'The Hammer,' because of the merciless way in which he smote the enemy" (*Catholic Encyclopedia*, vol. III, pp. 626 ff).

8. B. Born in Belgium in 1599 and died in Rome at the age of 22 in 1621. "What . . . distinguished him most from his companions was his piety. When he was hardly seven years old, he was accustomed to rise early and serve two or three Masses with the greatest fervor. He attended religious instructions and listened to Sunday sermons with the deepest recollection, and made pilgrimages to the sanctuary of Montaigu . . . reciting the [R]osary as he went, or absorbed in meditation. As soon as he entered the Jesuit college at Mechlin, he was enrolled in the Society of the Blessed Virgin, and made a resolution to recite her Office daily. . . . On Fridays, at nightfall, he would go out barefooted and make the Stations of the Cross in the town. Such fervent, filial piety won for him the grace of a religious vocation. . . . John offered the type of the saint who performs ordinary actions with extraordinary perfection. In his purity, obedience, and admirable charity he resembled many religious, but he surpassed them all by his intense love for the rules of his order" (*Catholic Encyclopedia*, vol. VIII, p. 450). He died of a sudden illness. Pope Leo XIII canonized him in 1888.

9. C. 521-597 and 1303-1373, respectively, St. Columba founded monasteries and churches all over Scotland, and while most of

what we know about St. Brigid is legend (including her miraculous changing of water into beer for a leper colony), we know she founded several abbeys and communities as well.

10. E. First, what's the deal with all the initials instead of using first names? Second, old J.R.R. (1892-1973), affectionately called "JRT" (pronounced "jirt") by his friends, was never Anglican. His Baptist mother converted to the Catholic faith when he was a child – and later in life, he wrote a couple of books you might have heard about.

11. B. "A monk of the Order of St. Benedict, b. near Paris circa 995; died at Avellano, 1050. He invented the system of staff-notation still in use, and rendered various other services to the progress of musical art and science" ("Guido of Arezzo," *Catholic Encyclopedia*, vol. VII, p. 65).

12. A. True story. "Pope (236-250), the extraordinary circumstances of whose election is related by Eusebius (*Church History*, VI.29). After the death of Anterus he had come to Rome . . . from his farm and was in the city when the new election began. While the names of several illustrious and noble persons were being considered, a dove suddenly descended upon the head of Fabian, of whom no one had even thought. To the assembled brethren the sight recalled the Gospel scene of the descent of the Holy Spirit upon the [Savior] of mankind, and so, divinely inspired, as it were, they chose Fabian with joyous unanimity and placed him in the Chair of Peter. During his reign of fourteen years there was a lull in the storm of persecution. Little is known of his pontificate" ("Pope Saint Fabian," *Catholic Encyclopedia*, vol. 5: p. 742).

Bears Beat Boys and Battlestar Galactica

Some stories in the Bible are truly astonishing and unexpected. Here's one of them as well as 11 other interesting aspects of the Catholic Faith.

1. Who was mocked for being bald by a pack of rowdy boys but had the last laugh on them?
    a. Zechariah
    b. Elisha
    c. Paul
    d. Jacob
    e. Mike Ehrmantraut

2. What is a *baldacchino*?
    a. a rare form of male-pattern baldness
    b. a large, ornate canopy providing cover over the high altar
    c. an Italian nickname for Amazon founder Jeff Bezos
    d. the name for the top covering or lid of the ciborium holding consecrated hosts
    e. an herbal energy drink popular with many popes, especially in the mid-afternoon

3. Which beautiful young woman, at the instigation of her mother, danced seductively for the drunken King Herod and demanded from him the head of John the Baptist?
    a. Jezebel
    b. Herodias
    c. Salome
    d. Delilah
    e. She is not named in the Gospels

4. Which of these ecclesiastical punishments was threatened by early general and regional councils for clerics who refused to obey Church teachings?
    a. the "thorn paddle"
    b. banishment
    c. skunk-hair shirts
    d. being deposed from office
    e. b & d

5. At which council(s) did the Catholic Church formally define the doctrine of Purgatory?
    a. Vatican I
    b. Chalcedon
    c. Florence
    d. Trent
    e. c & d

6. The African-Caribbean word "*voodoo*" means:
    a. zombie
    b. casting spells
    c. spirits
    d. magic
    e. a crudely conceived form of rural economics

7. The word "pagan" comes from the Latin term *pāgānus* meaning what?
    a. false
    b. country person
    c. worshiper of false gods
    d. hedonist
    e. ancient religion

8. The Hebrew exclamation "Hosanna" means:
    a. save us, we pray
    b. joy to the world
    c. here he comes
    d. get that in your spirit
    e. praise God

9. Which of these is credited with having been the first to exclaim, "There but for the grace of God, go I"?
    a. St. Philip Neri
    b. King David
    c. St. Augustine
    d. The Good Thief on the cross
    e. St. John Henry Newman

10. The sin of acedia is more commonly known as what?
    a. lust
    b. wrath
    c. theft
    d. greed
    e. sloth

11. Which of the following is not one of the Seven Deadly Sins (but it's still bad)?
    a. avarice
    b. gluttony
    c. sloth
    d. not listening to *The Patrick Madrid Show* on Relevant Radio
    e. lust

12. According to St. Paul's Epistle to the Philippians, Euodia and Syntyche were:
    a. two of the first "deaconesses"
    b. two quarreling women in the church in Philippi
    c. two virtuous sisters who were martyred for the cause of Christ
    d. no one knows
    e. none of the above

Answer Key

1. B. Clearly, the Prophet Elisha was not someone you'd want to trifle with. 2 Kings 2:23-24 says: "He went up from there to Bethel; and while he was going up on the way, some small boys came out of the city and jeered at him, saying, 'Go up, you baldhead! Go up, you baldhead!' And he turned around, and when he saw them, he cursed them in the name of the LORD. And two she-bears came out of the woods and tore [mauled] forty-two of the boys.'"

2. B. Perhaps the most famous baldacchino (pronounced *ball-dah-KEE-no*) is the one standing above the high altar in St. Peter's Basilica in Vatican City (which itself stands directly above the subterranean chamber in which the bones of Saint Peter repose in a stone ossuary). Designed by architect Gian Lorenzo Bernini and completed in 1634, it soars nearly 100 feet into the air and took 11 years to complete.

3. E. Yes, that's true. She is nowhere named in the Gospel accounts of St. John the Baptist's martyrdom at the hands of Herod, although the Jewish historian Flavius Josephus (A.D. 37-100) names her as "Salome," the daughter of Herodias by her first husband Herod Philip before she left him and "married" Herod An-

tipas (See Matthew 14:6-8, Mark 6:22).

4. E. See 2 Thessalonians 3:13-14 and 1 Timothy 6:3-4. Even a cursory glance at the canons and decrees of the early ecumenical councils (the Council of Nicaea is a great example of the drama!) and regional synods shows how serious the Church was about requiring bishops, priests, and deacons to adhere to doctrine and important customs. Being deposed from one's ministry and reduced to the lay state was a very common consequence – less common was being struck dead (Acts 5).

5. E. The Councils of Florence 1431-1443 and Trent 1545-1563.

6. C. "Vodou, also spelled Voodoo, Voudou, Vodun, or French Vaudou, a traditional Afro-Haitian religion. Vodou represents a syncretism of the West African Vodun religion and Catholicism by the descendants of the Dahomean, Kongo, Yoruba, and other ethnic groups who had been enslaved and transported to colonial Saint-Domingue (as Haiti was known then) and partly Christianized by . . . Catholic missionaries in the 16th and 17th centuries. The word Vodou means 'spirit' or 'deity' in the Fon language of the African kingdom of Dahomey (now Benin)" (See *Encyclopedia Britannica*, "Vodou.")

7. B. The colloquial pre-Christian meaning of "pagan" (country person, civilian) carried no pejorative religious connotations, but in the early Church a "pagan" became synonymous with non-Christians, i.e., the unbaptized, heathens, and in a particular way those who worship false gods, e.g., of Rome and Greece. ("Paganism," *Catholic Encyclopedia*, vol. XIV, p. 578).

8. A. Catholics are familiar with this Hebrew word from the "*Sanctus, sanctus, sanctus*" prayer at Mass, which in English reads: "Holy, holy, holy, Lord, God of hosts. Heaven and earth are filled with Your glory. Hosanna in the highest. Blessed is He who comes in the name of the Lord. Hosanna in the highest." This is a

quote from Isaiah 6:3 and appears on the lips of those who followed Jesus during His earthly ministry (see Matthew 21:9, Mark 11:9, John 12:13).

9. A. (1515-1595) Born in Florence, Italy. "Did not Philip Neri say to Philip, as he saw a criminal haled to execution: 'There thou goest, Philip, but for the grace of God! And if thou hast escaped all these things, and the many more too numerous to mention, go down on thy knees, and thank thy God for His mercies!'" (*The Dolphin*, vol. III, p.68, January 1903).

10. E. From the Greek ἀκηδία (*akédía* = "lack of care or grief"), typically characterized as a distinctive listlessness or aimlessness in one's faith practice (or practice in general).

11. D. *Catechism of the Catholic Church*, 1866: "Vices can be classified according to the virtues they oppose, or also be linked to the capital sins which Christian experience has distinguished...called 'capital' because they engender other sins, other vices. They are pride, avarice, envy, wrath, lust, gluttony, and sloth or acedia." As far as I'm concerned, answer D is close to the edge.

12. B. See Philippians 4:2.

Was a Beatle Baptized Catholic? Get Back to Where You Once Belonged!

Here's a grab-bag of fascinating facts, biblical names, significant places, and even a few famous personages whose presence in this book might surprise you!

1. Where did Jesus change Simon's name to Peter?
    a. The Mount of Olives
    b. Caesarea Philippi
    c. Caesarea Maritima
    d. Capernaum
    e. Jericho

2. What did the Lord say when the Israelites made the golden calf while Moses was receiving the Ten Commandments?
    a. Behold! This is a stiff-necked people.
    b. Behold! What part of monotheism do you people not understand?
    c. Behold! You don't want that on your karmic record. No, you really don't.
    d. Behold! Because you have done this, cursed are you more than all cattle, and more than every beast of the field.
    e. None of the above.

3. Which biblical personage exclaimed the original "*Nunc dimittis, Domine*" ("Now dismiss [your servant], Lord"):
    a. Anna the Prophetess
    b. Moses
    c. King David

INQUIZITION

    d. Simeon the Prophet
    e. Nobody actually said that. It's a pious legend attributed to Zechariah, father of John the Baptist.

4. What does the biblical title "Son of Man" mean as Jesus used it?
    a. Son of God
    b. the Messiah
    c. first among equals
    d. Son of Justice
    e. here comes the Son

5. Okay, what does the biblical title "Son of God" mean as it was said of Jesus in the Gospels?
    a. of similar substance with the Father
    b. I am He
    c. the glory of God is upon me
    d. He is the literal Son of God
    e. God is my father figure

6. Who is the patron Saint of Madrid?
    a. Santiago (St. James the Greater)
    b. St. Teresa of Jesus
    c. St. Isidore the Worker
    d. St. Ferdinand III
    e. As anyone will tell you, it's definitely *not* Patrick Madrid, but in a parallel universe, wouldn't that be *wild*?

7. On which island did St. John the Apostle spend his final years in exile?
    a. Patmos
    b. Crete
    c. Capri

d. Malta
e. Washington Island

8. The Cathari (Catharists), a medieval heretical group in Europe, were best known for what bizarre practice?
    a. a refusal to take oaths
    b. starving some people to death
    c. dancing in the moonlight; they didn't bark and they didn't bite, they kept things loose, they kept things light
    d. calling out, "Goodnight, mama. Goodnight, daddy. Goodnight, Jim Bob. Goodnight, Mary Ellen. Goodnight, Johnboy," each evening before going to bed.
    e. a & c

9. What is *Mahershalalhashbaz*?
    a. Gibberish
    b. an untranslatable exclamation the Israelites grumbled against Moses while wandering through the desert
    c. The longest name in the Bible
    d. The name of the Witch of Endor whom King Saul asked to conjure the spirit of the Prophet Samuel
    e. A word you definitely do *not* want to mispronounce when ordering food at a Middle Eastern restaurant

10. Which imperial document granted religious liberty and legal status to Christians in the Roman Empire?
    a. Magna Carta
    b. Diet of Worms (*yuck!*)
    c. Edict of Milan
    d. Protocols of Constantine
    e. Edict of Toleration

11. Which of the Beatles was baptized Catholic?
    a. George and Paul
    b. Paul
    c. Ringo
    d. John and George
    e. all of them

12. No fair peeking: Which is the last book of the Old Testament?
    a. Amos
    b. Zechariah
    c. Habakkuk
    d. Nehemiah
    e. Malachi

Answer Key

1. B. See Matthew 16:13-19. There is a huge symbolic significance to this place as it is dominated by a massive rock cliff over 100 feet high, adorned with shrines to pagan gods, in the vicinity of which Jesus said of Simon Peter, "Upon *this rock* I will build *my church.* For all the fascinating details, see chapter two of my book *Pope Fiction: Answers to 30 Myths and Misconceptions about the Papacy* (patrickmadrid.com).

2. A. See Exodus 32:9 for the whole story.

3. D. See Luke 2:25-35, which we pray as a part of Night Prayer: "Now, Master, may you let your servant go in peace; for my eyes have seen the salvation, which you have prepared in the light of every people – a light of revelation to the Gentiles, and glory for your people Israel."

4. B. A term used by Jesus to identify Himself as the Messiah. "In the Old Testament 'son of man' is . . . employed as a poetical syn-

onym for man, or for the ideal man. . . . The Prophet [Ezekiel] is addressed by God as 'son of man' more than ninety times. . . . This usage is confined to [Ezekiel] except one passage in Daniel, where Gabriel said: 'Understand, O son of man, for in the time of the end the vision shall be fulfilled' (Daniel 8:17). The employment of the expression in the Gospels is very remarkable. It is used to designate Jesus Christ no fewer than 81 times — 30 times in St. Matthew, 14 times in St. Mark, 25 times in St. Luke, and 12 times in St. John" (*Catholic Encyclopedia,* vol. XIV, p. 144).

5. D. As Jesus declared, "I and the Father are one" (John 10:30) and "Have I been with you so long, and yet you do not know me, Philip? He who has seen me has seen the Father; how can you say, 'Show us the Father'?" (John 14:9). Even though, out of humility, Our Lord spoke of Himself as the "Son of Man," His followers (see Simon Peter, Matthew 16:16) and even enemies (sarcastically, in the case of Caiaphas Mark 14:61) referred to Him as the "Son of God" (see also Psalm 2:7). "That the Father, not the Son, had revealed [Christ's identity as the Son of God] shows how profound was the significance of Peter's words even if Peter himself had not yet fully sounded their depth. By this revelation the Father had singled out Peter as the natural foundation for His Son's society and Our Lord, as ever, follows His Father's lead. Faith in the divinity of Christ must henceforth be a criterion of the true society of Christ" (*A Catholic Commentary on Holy Scripture,* Dom Bernard Orchard, ed., Thomas Nelson and Sons, London, 1952, p. 858, 881).

6. C. (Not to be confused with Doctor of the Church St. Isidore of Seville, who lived 500 years earlier) Isidore the Worker was born in Madrid in 1070 and was, as his name implies, a humble layman and farm worker. His wife Maria, though less well known, was acclaimed for her life of holiness. If only we knew more about her! "Every morning before [Isidore went] to work he was accustomed

INQUIZITION

to hear a Mass at one of the churches in Madrid. One day his fellow-laborers complained to their master that Isidore was always late for work in the morning. Upon investigation, so runs the legend, the master found Isidore at prayer, while an angel was doing the plowing for him. On another occasion his master saw an angel plowing on either side of him, so that Isidore's work was equal to that of three of his fellow-laborers. Isidore is also said to have brought back to life the deceased daughter of his master and to have caused a fountain of fresh water to burst from the dry earth in order to quench the thirst of his master" (*Catholic Encyclopedia*, vol. VIII, p. 189).

7. A. Patmos, a small island off the coast of Turkey approximately 50 miles southwest of Ephesus, is where John finished his long life and was where he wrote the Book of Revelation. "I John, your brother, who share with you in Jesus the tribulation and the kingdom and the patient endurance, was on the island called Patmos on account of the word of God and the testimony of Jesus" (Rev. 1:9).

8. E. The Cathari, who were in certain ways doctrinally similar to the Waldensians and Albigensians, were dualists who embraced the Manichean heresy that spirit is good and matter is evil. Thus, they believed, our bodies are inherently evil and prone to sin, and thus they denounced marital intimacy as evil. "The Catharist system was a simultaneous attack on the Catholic Church and the then existing State. The Church was directly assailed in its doctrine and hierarchy. The denial of the value of oaths, and the suppression, at least in theory, of the right to punish, undermined the basis of the Christian State. But the worst danger was that the triumph of the heretical principles meant the extinction of the human race. This annihilation was the direct consequence of the Catharist doctrine, that all [sexual] intercourse between the sexes [i.e., married couples] ought to be avoided and that suicide, or the

Endura, under certain circumstances, is not only lawful but commendable. . . . no salvation was possible without previous renunciation of marriage" ("Cathari," *Catholic Encyclopedia*, vol. III, p. 437).

9. C. This name is given to Isaiah's son in Isaiah 8:3. (Hebrew: מַהֵר שָׁלָל חָשׁ בַּז [Ma'her-shal'al-hash-baz] = "hastening is [the enemy] to the booty, swift to the prey." Seriously. That's what it means. I'll bet Maher-shalal-hash-baz was the only kid with that name in his first-grade class.

10. C. A "proclamation that permanently established religious toleration for Christianity within the Roman Empire....the outcome of a political agreement concluded in Mediolanum (modern Milan) between the Roman emperors Constantine I and Licinius in February 313. The proclamation, made for the East by Licinius in June 313, granted all persons freedom to worship whatever deity they pleased, assured Christians of legal rights (including the right to organize churches), and directed the prompt return to Christians of confiscated property. Previous edicts of toleration had been as short-lived as the regimes that sanctioned them, but this time the edict effectively established religious toleration" (*Encyclopaedia Britannica*, "Edict of Milan").

11. A. Paul McCartney's mother Mary was Catholic and she had him baptized Catholic as an infant, though he no longer identified as Catholic from his youth onward and by 1965 identified as an agnostic (see *Paul McCartney: The Lyrics*, vol. 2, p. 414). George Harrison was baptized in 1943 at Our Lady of Good Help Catholic Church (see "Church where Beatle George Harrison Was Baptised in Is to Be Closed," *Liverpool Echo* (liverpoolecho.co.uk). He too ceased identifying as Catholic from his youth onward and eventually became a Hare Krishna.

12. E. Okay, now you can look. It's right there at the end.

Light of the World, Life of the Party

Jesus' ministry certainly involved great suffering, profound revelations, and also moments of joyful celebration...Thankfully, in Scripture, the Mass, the Church's teachings and devotions, the Catholic Church keeps these truths alive in every generation, ever ancient, ever new, to the glory of God!

1. The Latin term *summum bonum* refers to what?
    a. life of the party
    b. grave sin
    c. supreme good
    d. correct arithmetic
    e. conjugal rights

2. The correct and original meaning of the Catholic abbreviation "IHS" is:
    a. In His Service
    b. One Holy Catholic
    c. the first three letters of the Latin "*Iesus Hominum Salvator*" (Jesus, Savior of Mankind)
    d. the first three Greek capital letters of the name "Jesus"
    e. the first three letters of the Latin "*Iesus Hierosolymōrum Salvator*" (Jesus, Savior of Jerusalem)

3. According to Catholic theology, the priest is said to celebrate the sacraments:
    a. *in persona Christi*
    b. *con mucho gusto*
    c. *magna cum laude*

d. *ex corde ecclesiae*
e. *per saecula saeculorum, amen*

4. The Latin phrase, *"per omnia saecula saeculorum"* means:
    a. thy will be done
    b. the reign of God is at hand
    c. the new world order is for all
    d. for ever and ever
    e. this is for all the lonely people

5. St. Jerome once remarked that the incredible power of St. Paul's words was like:
    a. peals of thunder
    b. lightning across the Mediterranean sky
    c. a stampede of wild horses
    d. the crash of ocean waves against a rocky cliff
    e. an earthquake

6. The Magi brought baby Jesus in the manger gifts of Gold, Frankincense, and?
    a. Pampers
    b. myrrh
    c. nard
    d. bitter herbs
    e. hyssop

7. According to the Gospels, Jesus' first public miracle was:
    a. walking on water
    b. causing a gigantic catch of fish for Peter, James, and John
    c. healing a leper
    d. the multiplication of the loaves
    e. changing water into wine

8. The *protoevangelium* can be found in this passage of Scripture:
    a. Genesis 1:1
    b. John 1:1
    c. John 3:16
    d. Exodus 20:5
    e. Genesis 3:15

9. How is the date for Easter determined each year?
    a. it is the day of Jewish Passover
    b. it is the Sunday before Mother's Day
    c. it is the first Sunday after the first full moon following the vernal equinox
    d. it is whatever date the pope chooses in any given year
    e. it is the first Sunday after the first green buds emerge on the trees

10. What worldview tends to embrace the notion of God as a watchmaker – a distanced creator Who created a universe that runs itself?
    a. Gnosticism
    b. Deism
    c. Pantheism
    d. Mechanicalism
    e. Chronologicalism

11. Which of the Twelve Apostles does Luke's Gospel say were present in the room when Jesus raised the daughter of Jairus?
    a. Peter and Andrew
    b. Peter, James, and John
    c. all of the Apostles except Judas
    d. all of them
    e. none of them

12. Which of these is *not* one of the four senses of Scripture?
    a. allegorical
    b. pedagogical
    c. moral
    d. literal
    e. anagogical

Answer Key

1. C. Ultimately, God is *the* supreme good. In created things that are deemed to be greater/lesser/the greatest, certain things are recognized as the "highest good" or "supreme good" in a given situation, such as "This is my commandment, that you love one another as I have loved you. Greater love has no man than this, that a man lay down his life for his friends" (John 15:12-13).

2. D. ΙΗΣΟΥΣ (JESUS) "Sometimes above the H appears a cross and underneath three nails, while the whole figure is surrounded by rays" (*Catholic Encyclopedia*, vol. VII, p. 649).

3. A. *Catechism of the Catholic Church*, 1548: "In the ecclesial service of the ordained minister, it is Christ himself who is present to his Church as Head of his Body, Shepherd of his flock, high priest of the redemptive sacrifice, Teacher of Truth. This is what the Church means by saying that the priest, by virtue of the sacrament of Holy Orders, acts *in persona Christi Capitis* [in the person of Christ the head]. 'It is the same priest, Christ Jesus, whose sacred person his minister truly represents. Now the minister, by reason of the sacerdotal consecration which he has received, is truly made like to the high priest and possesses the authority to act in the power and place of the person of Christ himself' (Pius XII, *Mediator Dei*: 39, 548)."

4. D. This Latin phrase, a common conclusion to many traditional

prayers, is an intensification of "*in saecula saeculorum*," which can be translated as "for ever and ever" or "throughout all ages upon ages."

5. A. "[T]he Apostle Paul's ... words seem to me, as often as I hear them, to be not words, but peals of thunder. Read his epistles... you will see how skillful and how careful he is in the proofs which he draws from the Old Testament, and how warily he cloaks the object which he has in view. His words seem simplicity itself: the expressions of a guileless and unsophisticated person -- one who has no skill either to plan a dilemma or to avoid it. Still, whichever way you look, they are thunderbolts" (Epistle 48, *To Pammachius*, 13).

6. B. Myrrh is mentioned 11 times in the Old Testament. Its Hebrew root word, *mor*, is "bitter." It was often used as one of the spices for embalming the dead, which is why it contributes to the mystery of the gifts to the infant Jesus – gold for a king, frankincense for a holy sacrifice, and myrrh for a burial.

7. E. See John 2:1-12. Although it's possible, though by no means likely, that the Lord performed one or more miracles privately before dramatically changing water into wine at the Wedding at Cana (a biblical example of "transubstantiation" no less!), this was his first recorded public miracle revealed to us in Scripture.

8. E. This passage is the *protoevangelium* (Greek = "first gospel" or "first good news") because God promises that through "the woman" (Mary), her "seed" (Jesus) will in due time literally "crush" Satan's head.

9. C. "[T]he solution adopted in 525 and in that officially put forward at the time of the reform of the Calendar by Gregory XIII, is this, that the Church throughout held that the determination of Easter was primarily a matter of ecclesiastical discipline and not of astronomical science. . . . According to this rule, Easter Sunday is

the first Sunday which occurs after the first full moon (or more accurately after the first fourteenth day of the moon) following the 21st of March. As a result, the earliest possible date of Easter is 22 March, the latest 25 April" (*Catholic Encyclopedia*, vol. V, pp. 229-230).

10. B. Deism as a concept arose in the 16th century and is a philosophical approach to understanding and attempting to account for the phenomenon of order and design in the cosmos that relies heavily on the observation of empirical data. British philosopher Samuel Clarke (1675-1729) classified deism into four categories or versions. Frederick Copleston, S.J., summarizes Clarke's views: "One version was proposed by those who acknowledged that God created the world but who deny that he plays any part in governing it. The second group consists of those who believe that all natural events depend on divine activity but who at the same time say that God takes no notice of man's moral behavior, on the ground that moral distinctions depend simply on human positive law. The third group consists of those who think indeed that God expects moral behavior from his rational creatures but who do not believe in the immortality of the soul. The fourth group consists of those who believe that there is a future life in which God rewards and punishes but who accept only those truths which can be discovered by reason alone.... [Deists] had a common belief in God, which differentiated them from the atheists, together with a disbelief in any unique revelation and supernatural scheme of salvation, which differentiated them from orthodox Christians.... they were rationalists who believed in God.... Some [deists] were hostile to Christianity while others were not hostile, though they tended to reduce the Christian religion to a natural religion" (*A History of Philosophy*, vol. V, pp. 157, 161-163).

11. B. See Mark 5:37

12. B. The *Catechism of the Catholic Church* explains that "one can distinguish between two [primary] senses of Scripture: the literal and the spiritual, the latter being subdivided into the allegorical, moral, and anagogical senses" (CCC 115). The allegorical sense is that which we can read events in the biblical text in relation to Christ's actions and our redemption; anagogical expands this to reading events in light of our eternal destination and salvation.

What's in a Name?

"The gatekeeper opens the gate for him, and the sheep listen to his voice. He calls his own sheep by name and leads them out."

—John 10:3

1. Jesus called these two disciples "Sons of Thunder":
    a. Peter & Andrew
    b. Peter & Paul
    c. James & John
    d. Aquila and Priscila
    e. Philip & Bartholomew

2. Which Catholic astronomer published his thesis on heliocentricity in 1543 and has been hailed as the father of modern astronomy since then?
    a. Galileo Galilei
    b. Tycho Brahe
    c. Gottfried Herder
    d. Nicolaus Copernicus
    e. Isaac Newton

3. St. Matthew's occupation before Christ called him as an Apostle was:
    a. physician
    b. scribe
    c. tent maker
    d. tax collector
    e. disciple of St. John the Baptist

4. Bartimaeus, a man mentioned in Mark's Gospel chapter 10, was noteworthy because he was:
    a. a leper
    b. a paralytic
    c. a magician
    d. a blind man
    e. a thief

5. Whose mother-in-law does the Bible say Jesus healed of a fever?
    a. the Roman Centurion
    b. St. Peter
    c. St. John
    d. St. James the Greater
    e. A guy with mixed emotions

6. The biblical account of Jesus changing Saul's name to Paul is found in:
    a. 1 Corinthians
    b. Acts
    c. Galatians
    d. Ephesians
    e. Jesus did not change his name from Saul to Paul

7. The term *Christian* was first used as a name for the followers of Jesus in:
    a. Rome
    b. Jerusalem
    c. Antioch
    d. Damascus
    e. No one knows for sure

WHAT'S IN A NAME?

8. How many times did Moses lead the Israelites around the City of Jericho before its walls crumbled?
    a. 7
    b. 77
    c. 7 times 77
    d. 3
    e. Is this a trick question? Very sneaky!

9. Which of these men mentioned in the Bible were twins?
    a. Moses and Aaron
    b. Abraham and Lot
    c. Ham and Shem
    d. Moe and Shemp
    e. Jacob and Esau

10. St. Matthew the Apostle is also known in Scripture as:
    a. Levi
    b. Strauss
    c. Jean
    d. Caleb
    e. Alpheus

11. Who was St. Peter's blood brother?
    a. St. Philip
    b. St. James
    c. St. Andrew
    d. St. John
    e. St. Matthew

12. Which disciple, being swifter, outran Peter on the way to Jesus's tomb on Easter Sunday morning?
    a. The Gospel does not name him
    b. James the Greater

97

c. James the Lesser
   d. Taylor the Swift
   e. John

Answer Key

1. C. See Mark 3:17. Jesus gave them this nickname because they were zealous and hotheaded (see Luke 9:54).

2. D. February 19, 1473 – May 24, 1543. "His great work, *On the Revolutions of the Celestial Bodies*, bears testimony to his unremitting observations of sun, moon, and planets. His reputation was such that as early as 1514 the Lateran Council, convoked by Leo X, asked through Bishop Paul of Fossombrone, for his opinion on the reform of the ecclesiastical calendar. His answer was that the length of the year and of the months and the motions of the sun and moon were not yet sufficiently known to attempt a reform. The incident, however, spurred [Copernicus] on as he himself writes to Paul III, to make more accurate observations; and these actually served, seventy years later, as a basis for the working out of the Gregorian calendar" ("Nicolaus Copernicus," *Catholic Encyclopedia*, vol. IV. pp. 352-353).

3. D. (Greek: *telōnēs*) Tax collectors were universally disliked by just about everyone. They were greedy, underhanded, and unmerciful. For Jesus to call one is a powerful showing of God's mercy *and* that each person has inherent goodness within them – sometimes it just takes Jesus calling you specifically to see it.

4. D. The really interesting thing about old Bartimaeus is that his enigmatic name can be translated either as "Son of He Who Is Highly Prized" (Aramaic: *bar* = "son of"; Greek: *Timaeus*, "highly prized") or "Son of Uncleanliness" (Aramaic: *bar* + Hebrew *tame* = "unclean" or "defiled").

5. B. See Matthew 8:14-15.

6. E. When God changed a man's name, it signified a profound change in his status and was a sign of his new mission. God changed Abram's name to Abraham (Genesis 17:1-7), Jacob to Israel (Genesis 35:9-12; see also Genesis 32:24-38), and Simon's name to Peter, meaning "Rock" (Aramaic: *Kephas*; Greek: *petros*) in Matthew 16:18, making him the first pope and promising to entrust to him the keys of the Kingdom of Heaven (John 1:42). See pages 21-50 in my book, *Pope Fiction: Answers to 30 Myths and Misconceptions about the Papacy*, for a great deal more on this issue.

7. C. See Acts 11:26, "it was at Antioch that they were first called Christians." According to St. Ignatius of Antioch's (d. 107) own usage, the term *Catholic* had, by the close of the apostolic era, become the most specific name for the Church Jesus had established.

8. E. See Joshua 6 for the whole story of how Joshua, not Moses, led the Israelites around Jericho.

9. E. See Genesis 25:24. The Apostle Thomas may also have been a twin; his Greek name Didymus means "twin," though his sibling is not named (John 11:16). Perez and Zarah were also twins, mentioned in Genesis 38:27-30. Of Cain and Abel, we cannot know from the time elapsed mentioned in Genesis 4:1-2 whether they were in fact twins or merely siblings.

10. A. Compare Matthew 9:9, 10:3 with Mark 2:14 and Luke 5:27. The Lord calling Matthew has inspired some incredible art, most notably "The Call of Matthew" from Caravaggio (1600), which stands alongside "The Inspiration of Matthew" (1602) and "The Martyrdom of Matthew."

11. C. See Matthew 4:18, 10:2

12. E. See John 20:2-6. The older I get, the more I understand the truth of this passage.

Are You Ready for Your Exit Interview?

The Protestant Reformation was Martin Luther's big break (from the Catholic Church)—think you can figure out these other solo careers?

1. *Lumen Gentium*, Vatican II's Dogmatic Constitution on the Church, states that "the one Church of Christ..."
    a. exists in the Catholic Church
    b. can be found in the Catholic Church
    c. is invisible and worldwide
    d. subsists in the Catholic Church
    e. is big, bad, and powerful

2. The term "soteriology" refers to:
    a. the science of designing churches and other sacred buildings
    b. the study of biblical genealogies
    c. the study of salvation
    d. a 4th-century heresy similar to the heresy of Scientology
    e. none of these

3. The judgment each person faces immediately after death is generally called by Catholics:
    a. final judgment
    b. particular judgment
    c. summary judgment
    d. exit interview (that's what *I* call it, anyway)
    e. a major bummer

4. Which of these figures of the Protestant rebellion was originally Catholic?
    a. Martin Luther
    b. John Calvin
    c. Ulrich Zwingli
    d. John Knox
    e. all of them

5. How many Lateran Councils were there (i.e., ecumenical councils held at the Basilica of St. John Lateran in Rome)?
    a. 1
    b. 2
    c. 3
    d. 4
    e. 5

6. The 1732 Royal Charter for the Colony of Georgia prohibited which of these things?
    a. dancing, smoking, and alcohol
    b. Catholics
    c. being intolerant
    d. all of the above
    e. none of the above

7. Which historical figure allegedly exclaimed, "Will no one rid me of this turbulent priest?"
    a. John Calvin
    b. King Henry II
    c. King Henry VIII
    d. Napoleon Bonaparte
    e. Nancy Pelosi

8. Which of these startling statements was made by Martin Luther:

a. "No sin will separate us from the Lamb, even though we commit fornication and murder a thousand times a day."
b. "Do not ask anything of your conscience, and if it speaks, do not listen to it."
c. "Be a sinner and sin boldly."
d. A and C
e. None of these

9. Which of these common Protestant beliefs is taught in the Holy Bible?
    a. *sola fide* (Latin: [justification] by faith alone)
    b. *sola Scriptura* (Latin: by Scripture alone)
    c. an absolute assurance of salvation (i.e., "once saved, always saved")
    d. all of them
    e. none of them

10. What term do the Eastern Orthodox Churches use for the sacrament of confirmation?
    a. extreme unction
    b. chrismation
    c. charismatic
    d. apocatastasis
    e. theosis

11. What is a Byzantine Catholic referring to when talking about his "eparchy"?
    a. priest
    b. diocese
    c. bishop
    d. prayer life
    e. a pesky rash common in Eastern Europe, Greece, and Turkey

12. C'mon now, 'fess up. Way down deep, which is your personal, all-time, really and truly *favorite* Relevant Radio Show?
    a. *Daybreak*
    b. *Morning Air*
    c. *The Patrick Madrid Show*
    d. *The Inner Life*
    e. *Fr. Simon Says*
    f. *The Drew Mariani (never heard of him) Show*
    g. *The Cale Clarke Show*
    h. *Trending with Timmerie*
    i. *The Family Rosary Across America with Father Rocky and Margaret Kleinschmidt*
    j. *The overnight re-run of the Patrick Madrid Show*
    k. ALL OF THE ABOVE

Answer Key

1. D. See *Lumen Gentium*, 8. Although there are clearer ways to say that the Catholic Church is that very Church Christ established, the phrase "subsists in," though seemingly ambiguous to the casual reader, is actually a direct statement. Dictionary.com defines "subsists" as "to have existence in, or by reason of, something, to reside, lie, or consist in" (the Catholic Church).

2. C. From the Greek word σωτήρ (*sotér*) = savior, deliverer.

3. B. "It is appointed for men to die once, and after that comes judgment (Heb. 9:27)."

4. E. See Hilaire Belloc's book *Characters of the Reformation* (Cavalier Books, 2018), which gives detailed biographical portraits of these and other significant figures in the Protestant rebellion against the Church.

5. E. Several of the early Lateran Councils addressed very similar issues. The First (1123) clearly prohibited "priests, deacons, subdeacons, and monks to marry or to have concubines," as did the Second (1139) in different words. The Third Lateran Council (1179) forbade "clerics to receive women in their houses, or to frequent, without necessity, the monasteries of nuns" and declared that the only group who could elect a pope would be a conclave of cardinals. The Fourth (1215) and Fifth (1512) Lateran Councils shake things up: the Fourth defined the dogma of Eucharistic Transubstantiation, urged the Greek Orthodox Church to return to the Catholic Church, and restricted clergy from "incontinence, drunkenness, the chase [i.e., hunting animals for sport], attendance at farces and histrionic exhibitions" (*Catholic Encyclopedia*, vol. IX, p. 16-19); the Fifth, just before the Protestant Reformation, reaffirmed the immortality of the soul and the decision-making authority of the pope, which had been previously questioned by discontent priests and cardinals.

6. B. "[We] grant, establish and ordain, that forever hereafter, there shall be a liberty of conscience allowed in the worship of God, to all persons inhabiting, or which shall inhabit or be resident within our said provinces and that all such persons, *except papists*, shall have a free exercise of their religion" (Yale Law School Avalon Project, "Charter of Georgia: 1732," avalon.law.yale.edu).

7. B. "'Will no one rid me of this turbulent priest?' (also expressed as 'troublesome priest' or 'meddlesome priest') is a quote attributed to Henry II of England preceding the death of Thomas Becket, the Archbishop of Canterbury, in 1170. While the quote was not expressed as an order, it prompted four knights to travel from Normandy to Canterbury, where they killed Becket" (Wikipedia, "Will no one rid me of this turbulent priest?")

8. D. Luther said a lot of strange and even bizarre things in defense

of his novel beliefs and in his frequent attacks on the Catholic Church. Even when read in context and with due allowances made for his penchant for hyperbole, many of his statements, such as the ones above, demonstrate how shocking some of his theological claims were, then and now.

9. E. Many Protestants are astonished to discover that, in spite of having been asserted confidently by men such as Luther and Calvin, the notion of "justification by faith alone" and "scripture alone," are actually nowhere taught in the Bible. I document this extensively in my books, *Answer Me This!* (Huntington IN, Our Sunday Visitor, 2003) and *Envoy for Christ: 25 Years as a Catholic Apologist* (Cincinnati, OH, Servant Books, 2012). See also *Surprised by Truth* (Basilica Press, 1994) for 11 powerful testimonies of former Protestants who, when through prayer and much study, discovered that those beliefs are not in fact biblical converted to the Catholic Church. See also my free articles on relevantradio.com/patrick – click "links," then "articles."

10. B. From the Greek word χρίσμα (*chrisma*) = "anointing, unction." See *Catechism of the Catholic Church*, 1242.

11. B. From the Greek word ἐπαρχία (*eparchia*) = "a sphere of duty, province" (*Strong's Exhaustive Concordance of the Bible*, G1885).

12. K is the only correct answer. Girl, you know it's true.

ABOUT THE AUTHOR

Patrick Madrid is the host of the daily three-hour "Patrick Madrid Show" on Relevant Radio, broadcast nationally on nearly 200 stations and globally on the Relevant Radio app.

His 26 books include *Life Lessons: 50 Things I Learned in My First 50 Years* (Ignatius Press), *How to Do Apologetics* (Our Sunday Visitor), and *Why Be Catholic? Ten Answers to a Very Important Question* (Random House) with a foreword by Cardinal Seán O'Malley, Archbishop of Boston.

For the past 35 years, Patrick has been a teacher of the Catholic Faith across many mediums: through his books and articles, on radio and television, and before live audiences in English and Spanish at his speaking events, across the country and around the world. He teaches as an adjunct professor of apologetics at Holy Apostles College and Seminary in Cromwell, Connecticut, and at St. Patrick's Seminary and University in Menlo Park, California. He also taught for several semesters on the theology faculty at Franciscan University of Steubenville.

He earned a bachelor's degree in business at the University of Phoenix, as well as a B. Phil. in philosophy and an M.A. in dogmatic theology at the Pontifical College Josephinum in Columbus, Ohio.

Married on February 7th, 1981, Patrick and his wife Nancy have been blessed with 11 children and 28 grandchildren. They reside in the Diocese of Columbus, Ohio. His website is patrickmadrid.com. Contact him on Twitter at @patrickmadrid.

relevant radio

Relevant Radio brings Christ to the world through the media, broadcasting 24/7 on over 194 stations in 42 states and across the world over the internet and the free mobile app. Relevant Radio owns and operates 109 stations and produces 89 hours of original programming each week.

Relevant Radio creates a community of hope. Through this personal and intimate forum of communications, marriages are saved, souls draw closer to Christ and His Church, and the Truth sets many free.

Mission Statement

Bringing Christ to the world through the media.

Guiding Principles

Faithful to the Magisterium and Catechism of the Catholic Church
United to the Bishops
Under the protective intercession of the Blessed Virgin Mary

Memorare Meter
Prayers to End Abortion

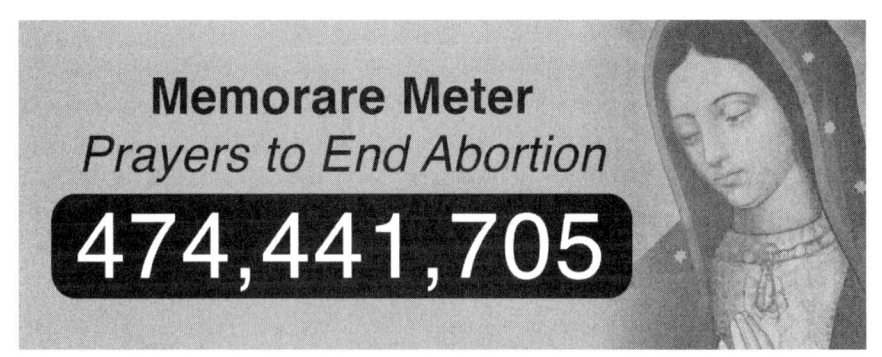

474,441,705

As of August 12, 2022.

Please join Relevant Radio in praying Memorares for the end of abortion. This is a most powerful prayer, and "this kind can only be cast out by prayer and fasting." (Matthew 17:20)

You can pray the Memorare yourself, or with friends, family, or with your class at school. Once you've accumulated 100 Memorares, visit www.relevantradio.com/mom so together we can track on our "Memorare Meter" and encourage others to pray more.

May God bless you and may Our Lady of Guadalupe, Protectress of the Unborn, hear our prayers!